Finn Juhl

FINN JUHL

Furniture · Architecture · Applied art

A biography by
ESBJØRN HIORT

THE DANISH ARCHITECTURAL PRESS 1990

The author would like to thank Hanne Wilhelm Hansen, who gave him access to Finn Juhl´s archives and collection of drawings, the latter now in the possession of the Museum of Decorative Art. The author would also like to thank the following for providing the financial means that made it possible to publish this book:
DANMARKS NATIONALBANK'S ANNIVERSARY FOUNDATION OF 1968
MARGOT OG THORVALD DREYERS FOND
MR. PAUL MAYEN, NEW YORK
NOVO'S FOND

© Esbjørn Hiort and Arkitektens Forlag, Copenhagen 1990
Illustrations editing and graphic design by Esbjørn Hiort
English edition translated by Martha Gaber Abrahamsen
Set in Baskerville at Hansen & Winther Fotosætteri
Reproduction by F. Hendriksen's Eftf. Reproduktionsatelier
3rd edition, 2nd print run
Printed: Scanprint A/S, Denmark

ISBN 978-87-7407-404-5

Contents

LIFE AND CAREER 7

FURNITURE 29
The Cabinetmaker's Guild exhibitions 31
Baker Furniture 34
Bovirke 38
France & Søn 38

INTERIORS 67
The Bing & Grøndahl store 67
The Trusteeship Council Chamber in New York 70
"Interior 52" in Trondheim 78
Villabyernes Bio 80
Ticket offices for SAS 82
DC-8 airplanes 84
The Wilhelm Hansen store 86
The Hotel Richmond restaurant 88

HOUSES 91
Finn Juhl's own house on Kratvænget 91
Villa Aubertin 98
Summer house in Asserbo 102
Summer house in Raageleje 104
Project for two houses in Klelund 106

EXHIBITIONS 111
Georg Jensen anniversary exhibition 111
"Home of the Future" at Forum 116
"The Arts of Denmark" in New York 118
"Two Centuries of Danish Design" in London 120

APPLIED ART 125

TROPHIES 135
The Kaufmann International Design Award 135
An "Export Oscar" 136

CONCLUSION 138

Finn Juhl – Curriculum vitæ 141
Finn Juhl's literary work 143
Writings about Finn Juhl 143

LIFE AND CAREER

Finn Juhl was trained as an all-round building architect, not especially as a furniture designer, something he himself considered important to emphasize. On several occasions, he pointed out that as a furniture designer, he was purely autodidact. His oeuvre did, however, also comprise a broad spectrum of architectural works. He made an especially excellent contribution as an interior designer. But it was nonetheless first and foremost furniture which made him a reputation, not only in Denmark, but internationally as well. And with good reason, since it was in this field that he showed truly original talent.

Finn Juhl designed his first furniture for himself. It is an old tradition for architects and painters to design furniture for their own use, one that in Denmark goes all the way back to the latter half of the 18th century, when the architect and painter Nicolai Abildgaard designed a number of pieces for his own use in a "neo-antique" style. There are various theories about why Abildgaard designed this furniture, which was inspired by scenes on Greek vases, cenotaphs, and sculptures. Some believed that he intended to use the pieces as models for his historical paintings, which depicted scenes from antiquity, while others cited political reasons. Neo-classical furniture was the style of the absolute monarchs, while furniture from antiquity originated in the times of the Greek and Roman republics. This is why this furniture came into fashion in the years following the French Revolution. Still others believe that Abildgaard simply wanted furniture that satisfied his aesthetic senses. Whatever the case, it became a tradition for painters and architects to design furniture for their own use. In the beginning of the following century, the sculptor H.E. Freund designed his own neo-antique furniture, as did M.G. Bindesbøll, who built the Thorvaldsen Museum, and many others throughout the century. In the beginning of our own century, the painter Johan Rohde designed some fine, simple pieces of furniture for himself and for friends and acquaintances, so it was indeed a strong tradition.

This furniture designed by artists is now found in museums, while the pieces which Finn Juhl designed for his own use will hardly become treasures. His later and best models, in contrast, now stand in museums of decorative art throughout Europe, the United States, Australia, and Japan. But they are not just museum pieces: they also stand in many private homes and public premises all over the world.

Finn Juhl was born on January 30, 1912, in Frederiksberg, part of Greater Copenhagen. His father, Johannes Juhl (1872–1941), was a textile wholesaler who represented a number of English, Scottish, and Swiss textile companies in Denmark. He never knew his mother, née Goecker, who died only three days after his birth. There is no

Finn Juhl photographed by Rigmor Mydtskov at his design office on Sølvgade in 1958.

way of knowing what this meant for Finn Juhl's childhood, but he himself denied that he missed her, for the logical reason that you cannot miss what you do not know. He had many friends whose mothers took tender care of the motherless boy. He himself felt that it perhaps made him more independent than he would otherwise have been. He was supported by his brother Erik, 2 years older, who was close to him throughout his life.

Finn Juhl noted in an interview that his relationship with his father was not especially warm. "Father was authoritarian, but I learned quite early that if I just obeyed him, nothing would happen to me – then I would have the rest of my time to myself... When my father came home before dinner, we had to tell him if we wanted to have an audience with him. And so he sat down at his player piano, his cigar in his mouth, and stamped out a classical repertoire, while I sat in a rocking chair with an antimacassar beside an imitation fireplace which had a large clock with a glass dome and General de Meza on horseback."[1]

Home could not have inspired Finn Juhl in his later work as an architect. "I grew up in a Tudor and Elizabethan dining room, and we had leaded windows and high panels. On the other hand, there was a Swedish chandelier in the living room. The study had Chesterfield chairs."

Finn Juhl said the following about his choice of career: "I wanted to be an art historian. I frequented the Royal Museum of Fine Arts from the time I was 15–16 years old; it was open one evening a week. And I was given permission to borrow books from the Glyptotek [museum] library by Frederik Poulsen, who was a Hellenist, while I am more enthralled by Achaean-Greek art. My practical father, who had an instinct for mammon, did not think that art history was a means of making a living. So we made the compromise that I would begin at the Academy, and I had the sinister ulterior motive that of course I would be able to study art history there at the same time."

After graduating from Sankt Jørgens Gymnasium in 1930, Finn Juhl was indeed accepted at the Royal Academy of Fine Arts' School of Architecture at Charlottenborg. At the time, the school was divided into a preliminary school, which consisted of two classes, and a main school, which consisted of three. The third and final class ended with a graduation project. Students normally spent their first two four-month summer vacations apprenticed to a mason or a carpenter, and the following summers at an architect's office. Working at an architect's office was an especially important part of a student's education. This is how he learned what the life of an architect was like in practice. But it was not easy to get a job at an architect's office, since the 1930s experienced one of the construction crises that have plagued architects in all ages. But Finn Juhl was lucky: in the summer of 1934, he got a job with the architect Vilhelm Lauritzen.

It was usually possible at the main school to choose one's professor, and Finn Juhl chose Kay Fisker. This proved a good choice, for he grew to admire Fisker as an architect. As things were, students did not have a close relationship with professors. All were practicing architects and also had large offices to manage. But they assigned projects and directed the teaching through assistants. In the course of a school year, the professor arrived two or at most three times and sat down at the student's drawing board to look at the project with which he or she was in progress and give some good advice. The as-

Finn Juhl stopped attending the Academy of Fine Arts' School of Architecture in 1934 and was then employed for 11 years by the architect Vilhelm Lauritzen. He was one of Lauritzen's closest collaborators on the Radio House, one of the first examples of true functionalism in Denmark.

When the Radio House's large concert studio was completed in 1945, Finn Juhl left Vilhelm Lauritzen's design office to start up his own practice.

The design office at 33 Nyhavn was not big – only c. 40 sq. m. – but it was cozy.

sistants also worked as architects so there were limits to how much students saw them. Actual teaching took the form of an overall critical review of how well the students had carried out their projects and of lectures given by both professors and teaching assistants. Kay Fisker was an excellent lecturer – something that could not be said of all the professors. Only Steen Eiler Rasmussen could match him, and perhaps Wilhelm Wanscher, who lectured on art history. Fisker's lectures were real attractions: a student had to be very ill indeed not to attend. He was probably the first lecturer at the Academy to show two slides on the screen simultaneously to provide a complement or a contrast. This made the lectures exciting, and Fisker's slide collection seemed inexhaustible.

In addition, Fisker was a fine architect. In 1931, he had (together with Povl Stegmann and C.F. Møller) won the Århus University competition, and in doing so created a Danish version of international functionalism, which was highly admired, especially by his students. On the whole, he markedly influenced his students' concept of architecture despite their sporadic personal contact. This was true especially in the case of Finn Juhl.

Vilhelm Lauritzen had been a teacher at the School of Architecture since 1926. Like Kay Fisker, he had a large private practice, which meant that his word was respected at the school. In 1934, he was given the major commission to build the Danish Broadcasting Corporation's Radio Building (*Radiohuset*), and in 1936, he won the competition for Kastrup Airport. These were modern commissions without any precedents in Danish architecture, and his designs compelled great respect. They were also major projects which required qualified personnel.

Like the professors, the teachers who had private practices also took advantage of the opportunity to hire the brightest students for their offices. The fact that a student was hired by Fisker or another professor said almost more about his abilities than his grades did. And so when a prominent teacher like Vilhelm Lauritzen chose Finn Juhl, we can judge the latter's qualifications as an architect. It was first intended as a summer job, but he continued at the office for eleven years. During the whole planning phase and construction of the Radio Building, Finn Juhl worked together with a colleague, Viggo Boesen, Vilhelm Lauritzen's closest associate at the office.

This meant that he never graduated, but that was not important, since he was accepted as a member of what is now the Federation of Danish Architects in 1942.

1930, when Finn Juhl began studying at the Academy, was the year when Gunnar Asplund's famous Stockholm Exhibition marked the breakthrough of international functionalism in Scandinavia. This major change in the conception of architecture did not take place in any particular year: it had been on the way since the beginning of the 1920s. In reality, it was an epoch-making revolution in architecture. Since the middle of the previous century, all architects had worked in historic styles: gothic, baroque, renaissance, and classicism, called "historicism." People were able to work "à la carte," as it were. It was even possible to combine several styles, through "eclecticism," a method which many architects detested. At around the turn of the century, people were getting tired of all this, and within a short span of time efforts were made to create a new nonhistoric style, *Jugendstil* in German and *art nouveau* in French. But it never really won a foothold in Scandinavia. It was succeeded here by a neoclassical period, which started in around 1910 and lasted for the next two decades.

Functionalism meant a decisive break with all historical styles. It meant a break with the classical conception of a building that was found in all styles: the house as a block, built on a symmetric plan with doors and windows as holes placed symmetrically in the facade. Functionalism released the straitjacket of symmetry. (The postmodernist architects of the 1980s again seem to have accepted it voluntarily.) Asymmetry became a principle which permitted a freer form for buildings in accordance with their function – which is where the term functionalism originates. The reason was that modern industrial society involved so many new, diverse tasks that a freer forming of buildings in this way had become necessary. In addition, new materials and building methods – especially reinforced concrete – opened completely new constructive potentials.

All architects – including Kay Fisker and Vilhelm Lauritzen – had been classicists in the period up to 1930. But the new idiom gained ground with unbelievable speed. The Radio Building, in particular, which Finn Juhl was to work on, emerged as an elegant and serene example of the new architecture. It has all of functionalism's typical characteristics: the clear geometrical construction forms, the flat roof, which is used partly for a garden, the continuous band of windows, the clear division into elements determined by function, the horizontal accentuation, the marked emphasis of smooth wall surfaces, the outer contour of the concert hall, reflecting its inner form. Attention to function was a leitmotif in the design, and this is expressed in many ways in the facade – not as dissonances, but on the contrary as carefully calculated architectonic effects.

Work at the Radio Building's design office was undoubtedly exceptionally stimulating for Finn Juhl. The building's interiors were worked out to the last detail, right down to the door handles and coatracks. It seems possible to trace Finn Juhl's sensitive design in many of these details, for example the lighting fixtures. Finn Juhl used many of them in his later interior design projects, but always emphasized that they were designed by Vilhelm Lauritzen. He mentioned to the author on one occasion that he had not designed the Radio Building's furniture, something that one could be led to believe since it was during his years at the Radio Building design office

STRÜWING

Finn Juhl made his debut as a furniture designer at the Cabinetmakers' Guild exhibition in 1937. He participated in 24 of these exhibitions, and his furniture won prizes in 16 Guild competitions. The picture is from the exhibition in 1950, where his pieces included a chair he had designed for the U.N. See the drawing on page 75.

Interior of cabinetmaker Niels Vodder's stand at the Cabinetmakers' Guild exhibition in 1951. The chair is the second of two designed by Finn Juhl for the U.N. See the drawing on page 77.

MAARBJERG

BRIGITTE UHRMEISTER

The cabinetmaker Niels Vodder, with whom Finn Juhl collaborated on the Cabinetmaker's Guild exhibitions for 22 years. He made all of Finn Juhl's best furniture.

that he made his breakthrough as a furniture designer.

In 1941, the Radio Building's administrative offices and studios were completed , but not until 1945 was the large concert hall ready. The work could have been finished earlier, but was dragged out intentionally. This was during the German occupation of Denmark, and it was feared that the Germans would confiscate the hall and make undesirable use of it as soon as it was ready.

When the Radio Building was completed, Finn Juhl resigned and founded his own office. His apprenticeship was over.

When Finn Juhl reached the age of 21, a sum that had been deposited with the public trustee's office – probably an inheritance from his mother – was paid to him. This gave him enough economic independence to enable him to move away from home. The change suited him admirably. He rented a modest apartment for which he designed his first furniture. It was a rarity in those days for a student to have his own apartment, and with handcrafted furniture he himself had designed. It was long before such concepts as state education grants, rent subsidies, and social welfare had been discovered. His friends at the Academy lived at home or in rented rooms around town. There were no dormitories for students of architecture.

Finn Juhl had his furniture made by a young cabinetmaker named Niels Vodder. This was the beginning of a long and fruitful period of collaboration between a creative architect and an excellent craftsman.

Finn Juhl made his public debut as a furniture designer at the Copenhagen Cabinetmakers' Guild exhibition at the Museum of Decorative Art in 1937. It was the Guild's 11th exhibition. Back in 1927, the Guild cabinetmakers had already taken up the struggle against the growing furniture industry by holding an annual sales exhibition, to begin with at the Institute of Technology, later at the exhibition premises (which, however, were remodeled in 1937 and made into the Palladium movie theater) of what is now the Federation of Danish Industry. The exhibitions were then held at the Museum of Decorative Art until they were discontinued in 1966, with the exception of a single year at the Charlottenborg exhibition hall (1938).

Before the annual exhibition, the Guild held a competition to find new types of furniture. It was an ingenious idea, since at relatively little cost the field was regenerated, something that was sorely needed. What people did not foresee was that the furniture industry, which was highly conservative, would later take advantage of this regeneration – completely free of charge. The demise of handcrafted furniture was, however, postponed for twenty or thirty years, to the great benefit of Danish furniture design.

The competitions brought out many talented young furniture designers, not because the prizes were especially large, but because the entries that won prizes – and often also those that did not – were presented at the year's exhibition. The opportunity to have one's ideas take form was what was so tempting. Finn Juhl won prizes in 16 of these competitions, in several cases first prize. He took part in 24 of the annual exhibitions, in 22 together with Niels Vodder, in two with the cabinetmaker Ludvig Pontoppidan.

Finn Juhl's furniture was a topic of discussion right from the beginning. "Most visitors will probably think that the whole room is

GUTENBERGHUS

Designing the Bing & Grøndahl store on Amagertorv Square in Copenhagen was Finn Juhl's first major interior design commission. The picture shows the portal of Oregon pine which marked the transition between the front part of the store and the exhibition area behind it. See also page 67.

very strange indeed, but with its potential for evoking discussion and jolting conservative conceptions, it is of great value," wrote the periodical Arkitekten of a living room designed by Finn Juhl in its review of the exhibition in 1939.[2]

The furniture designers who made their mark at the Guild's exhibitions in this period had either been trained as joiners or else had studied at the Academy's School of Architecture under Kaare Klint. But Finn Juhl had done neither. He was, as he himself said, autodidact. As will be discussed later (page 29), he broke with the tradition of craftsmanship within furniture design in a number of decisive ways. "Without overshadowing the merits of others, Finn Juhl's work should be emphasized as what in our time has had the greatest importance of all for the further development of furniture design in Denmark. He dared to break the firmly established Klint school's might and in doing so opened up the way for a new vigor, for movement," wrote Henrik Sten Møller forty years later in a review of Finn Juhl's retrospective exhibition at the Museum of Decorative Art (1982).[3]

Even if in the beginning there was little acceptance of Finn Juhl's furniture designs, recognition did come fairly quickly. Just ten years

DALE ROOKS

In 1951, Baker Furniture, Inc., Grand Rapids, Michigan, started producing Finn Juhl's furniture. The very next year, the models were presented in a showroom that he designed.

Finn Juhl's own house on Kratvænget in Ordrup photographed right after it was built in 1942. The decorative tree in the foreground later had to be felled because of age.

after his debut, he also began to work for the furniture industry. It was a farsighted man, Poul H. Lund, manager of Bovirke, who contacted Finn Juhl and suggested that his furniture be mass-produced. The result was quite large-scale manufacture. Later he collaborated successfully with the English-born manufacturer C.W.F. France, of France & Søn, and with several other furniture makers. A special chapter in his career was his work with Baker Furniture Inc. of Grand Rapids, Michigan, which manufactured his furniture in the United States beginning in 1951 (page 34).

In 1946, when Finn Juhl stood at the peak of his career as a furniture designer, he was given his first major interior design commission: the Bing & Grøndahl store on Amagertorv Square (page 67). The porcelain manufactory, founded in 1853, had a long and fine tradition of collaboration with creative artists. And so it was not strange for a promising young architect to be chosen when the company's sales outlet was to be remodeled. It was nonetheless a bold choice, since Finn Juhl was a controversial figure and it was his first important project of this type. The company management's selection was vindicated: the project proved one of Finn Juhl's main creations. The year after, it was awarded the Eckersberg Medal by the Academy Council.

Unfortunately it no longer exists, since in 1979 the store was remodeled, this time by another architect.

In 1937, Finn Juhl married the dentist Inge-Marie Skaarups, who was the same age as he and was equally interested in modern art. Their combined income made it possible for them to build their own house in 1942 on Kratvænget in Ordrup, north of Copenhagen (page 91). It was gradually filled with work by the Danish artists of the day: Vilhelm Lundstrøm, Svend Johansen, Egon Mathiesen, Else Fischer-Hansen. Richard Mortensen, Egill Jacobsen, Tove Olafsson, Erik Thommesen, Robert Jacobsen, etc.

A cherished dream had come true. Finn Juhl had always seen his furniture as part of a spacial effect. He believed that furniture, applied art, and fine art should form an entity in a home. He now had the opportunity to carry out this idea in practice.

It was natural that the way his home took shape interested Finn Juhl intensely, since he had concentrated on designing furniture for a number of years. This was, however, something that interested most young architects: it was a sign of the times. Housing was a burning issue in the 1930s because of the housing shortage – and an acute one at that – that had arisen after the First World War. In 1922, a government subsidy system was established to promote housing construction, first and foremost high-rise housing. The system was revised and expanded in 1928 to cover inexpensive government loans for single-family houses. This meant that non-profit housing associations were able to build very large concentrated housing complexes. This was the age of big garden cities. At the same time, housing design was in transition. Functionalism had created the slogan about "light and air in the home," and this covered both high-rise apartments and single-family houses. At the same time, associations of applied arts urged industry to start producing "good things for everyday use."

At the Academy, teaching in the main school's first class had concentrated on how housing should take shape, and throughout the

'30s, a number of public competitions were held for apartment buildings and single-family houses.

Finn Juhl's later work gave some the impression that he was only interested in elite projects and showed very little interest in those with a social aspect, but this is not correct. In the 1940s, he took part in several of these competitions with a social dimension, for example together with his friend Ole Hagen in the competition for an old age home in Gentofte in 1939, where their entry was purchased, and in a competition for emergency housing in 1940, where they were awarded a prize for an entry for linked houses. In 1944, Finn Juhl participated on his own in a public housing competition for row houses in Randers.

It was Finn Juhl's belief that an architect should always work out the ways in which a plan could be furnished regardless of whether it was for high-rise apartments or a single-family house. In an article in Arkitekten, he showed that it was often impossible to sensibly furnish the usual plans in public housing.[4] "The large non-profit housing associations and their architects assume a major responsibility," he concluded, "because the construction of enormous complexes makes defects more fatal than if they were found in single-family housing. They should work together with specialists who can take part in the planning from the start, on the one hand, and help residents when the buildings are ready, on the other. This would primarily involve practical work and not influencing tastes."

The article, which was quite sharply formulated, gave rise to a controversy involving prominent leaders in public housing construction who were not especially sympathetic to Finn Juhl's views – strangely enough. But he was ahead of his time. Eventually it became common for non-profit housing associations to work out furnishing suggestions for apartment plans, and people could either follow or ignore them.

For a number of years – from 1945 to 1955 – Finn Juhl had the opportunity to do practical educational work in the field of home furnishing, since he served as a senior teacher at the School of Interior Design in Frederiksberg. It was a school that had been founded by a practical idealist, the architect Harald Willerup, who, like Finn Juhl, found that too little emphasis was placed on practical interior design when housing was being planned. Kitchens in new housing, in particular, were poorly thought out, in fact often downright impractical. This was long before the day of the fitted kitchen. This private school was later taken over by the Frederiksberg Technical School and still continues its work on a high professional level.

Finn Juhl collected his views on interior design in the little book "Hjemmets Indretning" (furnishing the home). His views were demonstrated in practice in the furnishing of his own house on Kratvænget in Ordrup. It was much admired and publicized not only in trade journals but also in weekly magazines. And so it is strange that nearly a decade went by before he was commissioned to build another single-family house. This was probably because he was known as a furniture designer and was categorized as such.

One day, however, a lumber dealer from Nakskov telephoned Finn Juhl and said he had a commission for him since his wife was a great admirer of his furniture. Finn Juhl later said that he misunderstood the man and thought that it was an interior design project. When he came to Nakskov and asked to see the house, the man burst out, "Are

ERIK HANSEN

Villa Aubertin on Nakskov Fjord was one of the few single-family houses that Finn Juhl designed. The picture shows the covered terrace facing south. See also page 98.

Finn Juhl always designed every last detail of his houses. The picture shows the kitchen at Villa Aubertin. It had a window towards the north, but also received southern light from high windows.

STRÜWING

United Nations headquarters in New York. The high building houses the Secretariat; the low building to the right houses the General Assembly. The three council chambers are located in the low building in the foreground facing the East River.

UNITED NATIONS

you crazy? You have to design it first!" That was just what Finn Juhl had wanted, and the result, "Villa Aubertin," was also unusually fine and meticulously designed, completely furnished with Finn Juhl's own furniture (page 99).

In addition to this house, Finn Juhl was only commissioned to design a studio-cum-house for his friends the sculptor Erik Thommesen and the weaver Anna Thommesen (1957), a house for a fish exporter in Esbjerg (1949), and a couple of summer houses (pages 102 and 104). There were naturally also a few projects that never materialized (page 106).

1951 was a memorable year for Finn Juhl: the year he made his entrance on the American scene. The 1950s were, in fact, his busiest years in every respect.

In the United States, United Nations headquarters in New York was about to be completed. The high Secretariat building and the General Assembly building were already being used, and it was time to furnish the low building along the East River for the permanent councils. The whole complex had been built by an international team of architects under the leadership of the American architect Wallace K. Harrison. One of the chief architects at the design office was the Danish-born American architect Abel Sorensen. He was responsible for furnishing the offices, which is why he took a trip around the world in 1947–48 to look at furniture and other fittings. He visited Denmark, too, where he met Finn Juhl, among others. In 1948, another leading American, Edgar Kaufmann, Jr., was also planning a study trip to Scandinavia, invited by the Scandinavian associations of applied arts. At the time, Kaufmann was curator of decorative arts at the Museum of Modern Art in New York. Before he left, he was given some good advice by Abel Sorensen, who said that he should meet Finn Juhl, whose work was pointing out new directions in furniture design.

Edgar Kaufmann, Jr., met Finn Juhl at "Den Permanente" (The Permanent Exhibition of Danish Arts and Crafts and Industrial Design), where his furniture was being exhibited, and the result was not only collaboration on exhibitions in the United States, but also a life-long friendship.

Edgar Kaufmann, Jr., was an usual person. He was born in 1910 with a silver spoon in his mouth, as the saying goes, since his father Edgar Kaufmann, Sr., was a member of the American plutocracy, the owner of a large department store in Pittsburgh. Edgar Kaufmann, Jr., was not, however, the typical heir to a large company. From his earliest years, he was more interested in art and architecture than he was in business. At the age of 17, he refused to start the usual American college education and instead went to Europe, where he studied in Vienna, Florence, and London. When he came home to the United States, he met the architect Frank Lloyd Wright by chance, and this meeting decided his future. In 1934, he was made a member of Wright's Taliesin Fellowship, a kind of master class in Spring Green, Wisconsin, for selected students from around the world, later to include Denmark's Jørn Utzon. Edgar Kaufmann, Sr., visited his son there and as a result commissioned Wright to build a country house in a forested area by a waterfall in Bear Run, Pennsylvania, which the family had owned for some time. This was "Fallingwater," probably one of Wright's most famous and pioneering building creations.

At his father's death in 1955, Kaufmann, Jr., inherited "Fallingwater," which he donated in 1963 to a foundation, together with 1,750 acres of forest and $500,000. The house is now open to the public.

Even though Edgar Kaufmann, Jr., never received a university education, he became one of his country's most respected architecture historians and was professor at Columbia University for many years. He was associated with the Museum of Modern Art from 1940, but his work there was broken off by the war. From 1942 to 1946, he served in the U.S. Army Air Forces. After the war, he resumed his work at the museum, where he became curator of decorative arts. Through exhibitions and the foundation of a collection of exemplary industrial design, he made a major contribution to convincing American industry of the importance of good design.

Kaufmann was captivated by the idea of modern industrially produced applied art which was able to measure up to handcrafted products in quality – though with different criteria – and which was affordable by all. He was, however, fully aware of the danger of vacuous industrially produced art. He was elitist by nature, and loved the exquisite and excellent in art and architecture. But perhaps for this very reason, he wanted everyday things to be exalted, through design, from the indifferent or mediocre to the excellent and inspiring.

He saw these efforts materialized in Finn Juhl's work, while he otherwise felt that Danish applied art at the end of the '40s was highly conservative and not as advanced as Sweden's. In the United States the concept *Swedish Modern* was used for the modern Scandinavian style. Not until the end of the '50s did *Danish Design* become a byword on its own.

FAIRCHILD PUBLICATIONS

Finn Juhl's first major exhibition commission was "Good Design" at the Chicago Merchandise Mart in 1951. It was so successful that it was shown at the Museum of Modern Art in New York that autumn. Finn Juhl photographed at the entrance to the exhibition in Chicago.

Edgar Kaufmann, Jr., and Finn Juhl photographed in 1977 on the Greek island of Hydra. They met in 1948 in Copenhagen, and became life-long friends.

Edgar Kaufmann, Jr., was a student of Frank Lloyd Wright, who built the famous country house "Fallingwater" for his father. The son inherited it, and Finn Juhl visited him here several times.

From 1950 to 1955, Kaufmann arranged a special stand, "Good Design," at merchandise mart in Chicago. The idea was naturally to present good utilitarian objects to American industry, whose worst excesses were seen in abundance at the fair. American furniture, in particular, consisted almost solely of imaginative copies of old styles. Kaufmann asked Finn Juhl to arrange the "Good Design" exhibition in 1951. It was his first major exhibition, and it proved so successful that it was shown the same year at the Museum of Modern Art in New York.

Edgar Kaufmann, Jr., gradually became a kind of unofficial ambassador of Danish design in the United States. He wrote a number of articles on Danish applied art in respected American journals, the first, in 1948, on Finn Juhl's furniture. In 1953, he helped Scandinavian associations of applied arts contact a number of American museums with a view to showing their joint traveling exhibition "Design in Scandinavia." Two years later, he again helped bring the exhibition "50 Years of Danish Silver" – a revised version of Georg Jensen's anniversary exhibition at the Museum of Decorative Art, designed by Finn Juhl, to a number of other museums (page 115). He was also responsible for creating a link with the Metropolitan Museum of Art in New York, where the major exhibition "The Arts of Denmark" – also under Finn Juhl's auspices – was shown in 1960 (page 118).

When Edgar Kaufmann founded the distinguished "Kaufmann International Design Award" that same year, he asked Finn Juhl to design a symbol to be given the award-winners as a lasting token when the award's $20,000 had been used up. Juhl fulfilled the commission by choosing an ancient Chinese symbol, the Yüan-Kuei, which the Chinese emperors gave as a mark of favor to deserving subjects. He set the object in a box of Japanese hinoki cypress with an inscribed silver plate (page 135). The first award was given to the famous American designers Charles and Ray Eames.

The friendship between Edgar Kaufmann, Jr., and Finn Juhl had a professional basis, since Kaufmann greatly respected Juhl as a designer and an architect, and Juhl, in turn, admired Kaufmann's vast knowledge and fine appreciation of art and architecture. Their correspondence shows that their friendship was fruitful for both.

They traveled together on several occasions to look at art, among other things to Italy in 1966, and Finn Juhl visited Kaufmann at Fallingwater, in New York, where Kaufmann had his permanent residence, and on the island of Hydra in the Greek archipelago, where he had a country estate. Kaufmann naturally also visited Finn Juhl on Kratvænget. Their friendship lasted throughout their lives. They died in 1989 within the space of a few months.

In 1950, Finn Juhl was chosen to furnish one of the large council chambers at United Nations headquarters in New York. He was selected by Denmark at the recommendation of the Academy Council, which had awarded him the Eckersberg Medal three years previously. This might seem completely natural, but he was nonetheless an unknown quantity as an architect, and at the U.N., he would be competing with two highly experienced architects from Norway and Sweden. Three meeting chambers were to be furnished for the U.N.'s three permanent councils: the Security Council, the Trusteeship Council, and the Economic and Social Council. The three Scandinavian countries, Denmark, Norway, and Sweden, had each undertaken to appoint an architect to carry out the work. It is impossible to say whether it was because Scandinavian design was much admired in the United States at the time or because Scandinavia had provided the United Nations with its first two secretary generals, the Norwegian Trygve Lie and the Swede Dag Hammarskjöld. The reason for the choice is probably more prosaic: each of the three countries had offered to pay the costs of furnishing its chamber.

Sweden chose the architect Sven Markelius, who at the time was 61 years of age and was one of Sweden's most respected architects. He was in charge of city planning in Stockholm and had a large private practice. Norway chose Arnstein Arneberg as the interior architect. He was 68 years old and was also a respected and experienced architect who had carried out major commissions, among other things designing Oslo City Hall (together with Magnus Poulsson).

Finn Juhl was only 38 years old and had never before carried out such a large public commission. It is thus natural to imagine that Finn Juhl had been mentioned by the Americans as a possibility, and if so it might have been Abel Sorensen and Edgar Kaufmann, Jr., who were responsible for this confidential recommendation..

Whatever the case, Finn Juhl was selected, and it proved a good choice. In an article, "Finn Juhl on the American Scene," Kaufmann later wrote the following: "Finn Juhl's Trusteeship Council Chamber is a resounding success. It surpasses its two companion efforts in establishing overall harmony, cheerful simplicity, and unstrained resourcefulness. Color and texture, the only elements of design left unimpeded to the interior architects, are handled by Juhl with Mozartian virtuosity and control. Natural woods and primary colors blend and accent a big composition of textural counterpoint, illuminated by sunlight and by lamplight both, delicately and precisely. The artificial illumination is better than that of any large meeting hall I know here in the United States; the natural light is as gentle as the building permits."[5] (Page 70).

In creating the Trusteeship Council Chamber at the United Nations, Finn Juhl had instantly become an international name, and this was probably why SAS contacted him in 1956 and asked him to design its

UNITED NATIONS

The Trusteeship Council gathered at a meeting in its chamber at U.N. headquarters in New York. Finn Juhl designed the chamber in 1951–52. It was difficult commission because of the room's inharmonious dimensions and the strong backlight from the large glass wall facing the East River. In spite of the difficulties, Finn Juhl's design for the project was brilliant. See also page 70.

The Trusteeship Council Chamber at the U.N. seen from the visitors' area. One can clearly see the highly unusual ceiling construction which gave the room its distinctiveness from the other two council chambers, one designed by a Swede, the other by a Norwegian architect.

UNITED NATIONS

ticket offices in Europe and Asia (but strangely enough not in the United States, where he otherwise had good contacts).

Scandinavia's airlines had started collaborating on flights to the United States back in 1946, and in 1950, this collaboration had been formalized with the founding of Scandinavian Airlines System. Since the company flew most international routes, SAS had to be given a public image. SAS was one of the first major enterprises to realize that design was the way to create the right one. It was an enormous project. No fewer than 33 ticket offices were designed within the course of a very few years (page 82). Some only had to be modernized, while most were completely new.

A problem which preoccupied Finn Juhl in his work on these ticket offices was their artistic decorations – or rather the lack of them. All major airlines were in the process of opening ticket offices in various major cities, and as a rule they were decorated with model airplanes, maps of the world with different routes drawn on them, travel posters, etc. Only KLM's ticket office on the Champs Elysée in Paris had a whole back wall two stories high covered with an Aubusson tapestry made by Jean Lurçat specially made for the purpose. "It looked completely nonsensical together with the shabby counter and bad furniture – but the overall idea was grandiose," noted Finn Juhl in one of his reports.

Finn Juhl recommended that SAS become the world's largest art

KELD HELMER-PETERSEN

patron! His reasoning was that distinctive furnishings were valuable as an expression of quality during the day, when there was life and movement in the office, but that they were not of any interest as such in the evening, when the rooms were empty, with lights on full force. They were boring as can be, just like a bank. If it had an excellent work of art to set in focus – a painting, a sculpture, or a tapestry – SAS would stand out from the other airlines. But two conditions had to be met: the work should be of the finest artistic quality and it should be made by a well-known artist in the country in question. He did not feel that Scandinavian artists could be used because their international position was too weak, and because their work reflected international trends too closely. The works of art should either be purchased by a committee of experts or commissioned especially for the offices in question. For the ticket office in Paris, he proposed a sculpture by Giacometti, who was living there at the time. Finn Juhl pointed out that a relatively large investment was required, but that it was an investment that would not decrease in value. (Considering the soaring price of art today, we must admit that Finn Juhl was right in this respect. It would have been an excellent investment.)

It is uncertain whether the recommendation was seriously considered at SAS, but in any case it was not acted upon. Either SAS did not believe in the project's value as advertising or else it boggled at making such a large investment. SAS was faced with major expenditures at the time as it made the changeover to jet planes. It had just ordered seven new Douglas DC-8s to replace propeller planes on long-distance routes. While a DC-7 cost nearly $2.7 million (with all spare parts) in 1956, a new DC-8 cost $8 million. It was an enormous sum of money at the time.

The new planes were to be delivered at the beginning of 1958, and Finn Juhl was commissioned to design their interiors. This was a new large-scale project that came at a time when he had his hands full. But he did an excellent job on this project as well (page 84).

SAS's ticket office in Gothenburg. Finn Juhl designed a total of 33 ticket offices for SAS in Europe and Asia. See page 82.

Finn Juhl also made his mark as an excellent exhibition architect in the 1950s. He had done his first important work in the field with "Good Design" in Chicago in 1951 and at the Museum of Modern Art in New York. When the Danish Society of Arts and Crafts was asked in 1952 to present a major representative exhibition at the Kunstgewerbemuseum in Zurich, he was asked to design it.

The Society played an important role in design during and after the Second World War. It was a powerful organization at the time since both individual craftsmen and major decorative arts enterprises were part of one body. Companies provided the financial resources for large-scale projects that would have been beyond the reach of the economically weak craftsmen on their own. The annual spring exhibition, which covered both categories of applied art, had a highly selective jury that created competition among craftsmen and – especially important – companies engaged in decorative art to produce utilitarian objects of the highest quality, both technically and aesthetically. It would hardly be incorrect to say that these exhibitions played a key role in making the 1950s and '60s a golden age for Danish applied art. It was also this concentration of forces that made possible the large exhibitions abroad which established Denmark's reputation in the field of applied art.

But the fact that both groups were represented also proved the Society's Achilles heel. There was a natural antagonism between the two groups which constantly surfaced, and which finally led to the demise of the Society. Nearly every exhibition – both at home and abroad – was followed by criticism. Craftsmen felt that they were being stifled by decorative arts, and felt that the jury compromised on artistic quality for commercial reasons. Industry, in turn, felt that the Society set standards too high and did not take enough account of the fact that products also had to be salable.

Antagonism came to a head in 1942 (when official Denmark was still bearing with the German occupation), when the Society managed to have a large official exhibition arranged in Stockholm. The exhibition was designed by the architect Mogens Koch and was an excellent manifestation of Kaare Klint's line within Danish ap-

KELD HELMER-PETERSEN

The many commissions for SAS made it necessary for the design office to move to larger premises at 38 Sølvgade. The office was set up in a former wine cellar, still fragrant with Bordeaux. The picture shows Finn Juhl's own office. In the background is a sculpture by Erik Thommesen, whose work was very often included in Finn Juhl's interiors.

plied art. Koch had been almost autocratic in his choice of pieces for the exhibition, which gave it a uniquely fine uniformity – but a lack of balance as well. It also gave rise to sharp criticism from the big decorative arts companies, among others the Royal Copenhagen Porcelain Manufactory, which was hardly represented at the exhibition. The clamor almost broke up the Society.

The same thing repeated itself – in more subdued fashion – when Kaare Klint himself arranged a large official exhibition, "Danish Art Treasures," at the Victoria & Albert Museum in London in 1948. As one could expect, it was a very elegant and harmonious exhibition, completely in Klint's style. The exhibition also covered older art and arts and crafts, so modern applied art was represented only to a limited extent. As a result, there was little criticism of this exhibition's lack of balance.

The fact that Finn Juhl was at the time considered an opponent of the Klint school was probably one reason why he was chosen to arrange the exhibition in Zurich. This did not mean that lower standards were set than heretofore, since Finn Juhl was not a man to compromise on quality. But it did mean that his choices were less one-sided.

The exhibition at the Kunstgewerbemuseum was not criticized, either: in fact it received universal praise.

The Society also chose Finn Juhl as the architect for the Danish stands at the Xth Milan Triennial in 1954 and the XIth Triennial in 1957. These international exhibitions of applied art and architecture were important in the post-war years. They were of a very high standard and the awards presented by an international jury in the form of diplomas and silver and gold medals were highly coveted – almost like today's Oscars in the movie industry. Scandinavia truly made its mark during this period. At the Triennial in 1957, Scandinavia captured around a third of all awards.

At the Triennial in 1954, Finn Juhl was awarded an honorary diploma for his design of the Danish stand and two gold medals for furniture. At the Triennial in 1957, he won a gold medal for his design of the Danish decorative arts section and once again two gold medals for furniture. This was quite an achievement, especially considering that competition in the field of design from larger countries – particularly Italy and the United States – had become fierce.

In the 1950s, it was quite clear that the United States was the target of the future for Danish exports, and many individual campaigns had been launched by the decorative arts to strengthen this trend. The largest project was conceived by the Scandinavian associations of applied arts in the form of a traveling exhibition, "Design in Scandinavia," which was shown at a number of museums throughout the United States in 1954–57. A competition was held to determine who was to be the exhibition's architect, and Finn Juhl naturally took part with a distinctive project as his entry. But he did not win. The winner was Erik Herløv – later professor of industrial design at the Academy of Fine Arts – with an ingenious system of showcases which served at the same time as shipping crates for the exhibition. But Finn Juhl arranged another traveling exhibition, "Neue Form aus Dänemark," which was shown in a number of German cities and in Vienna in 1956–57. Reconstruction in Germany was so far along that it was time to think of this market, too.

The largest Danish exhibition, however, was "The Arts of Den-

"The Arts of Denmark," shown at the Art Institute of Chicago, was opened by Prime Minister Viggo Kampmann. The exhibition had first been shown in New York, where it was opened by King Frederik IX. From the left, George B. Young, vice-chairman of the institute's board of trustees; Allan McNab, curator of the institute; Count K.G. Knuth-Winterfeldt, Denmark's ambassador to the United States; Prime Minister Viggo Kampmann, cutting the obligatory ribbon; and Anders Hostrup-Petersen, the primus motor of the exhibition. Finn Juhl can be glimpsed in the background on the left. See also page 118.

Finn Juhl naturally included his own furniture in the exhibitions of arts and crafts and decorative art that he designed abroad. At the exhibition "The Arts of Denmark," he showed e.g. this sofa bench, designed in 1948, and a panel wall. The chair in front of the panel wall was designed by Hans J. Wegner.

BENTE HAMANN

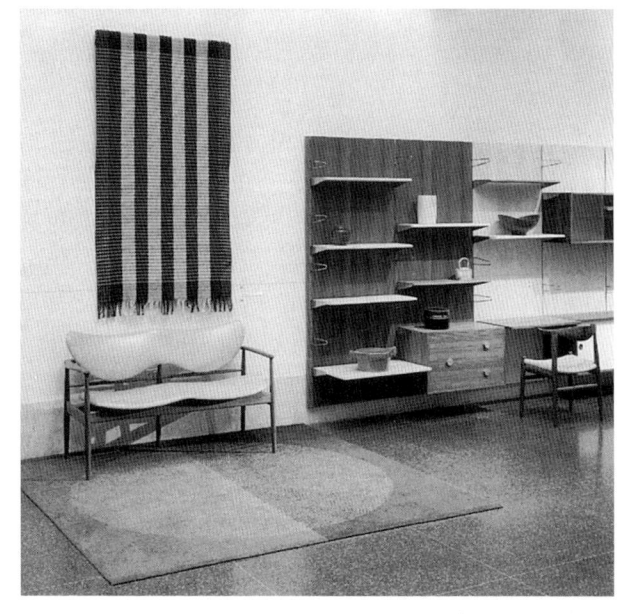

The exhibition "Two Centuries of Danish Design" was first shown at the Victoria & Albert Museum in London, where it was opened by King Frederik IX, and later in Glasgow and Manchester under the name of "A Century of Danish Design." In Glasgow it was opened by the Minister of Culture, K. Helveg Petersen, and in Manchester by the Foreign Minister, Poul Hartling. The picture is from the opening in Glasgow, where K. Helveg Petersen is addressing the distinguished guests. On the far right is Denmark's Ambassador, Erling Kristiansen, and on the far left, Finn Juhl. Third from the left is Anders Hostrup-Pedersen, the primus motor for the exhibitions in England and Scotland. See also page 120.

Interior from the exhibition at the Kelvingrove Museum in Glasgow. In the foreground is Finn Juhl's "Chieftain Chair," and in the background are chairs designed by Ole Wanscher and Kaare Klint. See also page 122.

mark," at the Metropolitan Museum of Art in New York in 1960 (page 118). Finn Juhl was the natural choice for this project in the United States, where his name was respected. The exhibition was part of a major Danish campaign in conjunction with the official visit of the Danish King and Queen. The visit aroused considerable attention, especially since King Frederik IX had the opportunity to speak to the United Nations General Assembly. It was during those unsettling days when the Soviet Union's Krushchev attended the session. During the debate, he became so incensed that he took off his shoe and banged it on the table and the General Assembly's undaunted president (who was an American) called him to order. A couple of days later, King Frederik attended a luncheon given in his honor by the City of New York. When the Mayor of New York mentioned the General Assembly's president in his welcoming address, King Frederik stood up and clapped, which naturally led all those present to rise and join in the ovation. The next day, New York's newspapers had headlines about Denmark's King standing up for the General Assembly's president!

The exhibition was exquisite, and it was a success, with 80,000 visitors – quite a figure, even by American standards. The number of visitors is naturally always important, but almost equally important is the coverage that a large exhibition like this one is given, not just in the dailies, but also in the major periodicals and trade journals. "The Arts of Denmark," which was later shown in Washington, D.C., and San Francisco, prompted extensive coverage of Danish applied art. "Danish design" became a byword in the United States during this period.

In addition to a few smaller-scale exhibitions for the Danish Society of Arts and Crafts throughout the 1960s, Finn Juhl once again arranged a major official Danish exhibition, this time in London in 1968. "Two Centuries of Danish Design" at the Victoria & Albert Museum was part of a Danish campaign in Great Britain. This time as well the royal couple graced the various arrangements, which included the Danish Royal Ballet's guest performances at the Royal Opera House, Covent Garden.

As in 1958, the exhibition also had examples of older art and arts and crafts, this time from the 19th century, but mostly as an introduction. It was the arts and crafts and decorative arts of our own time which dominated (page 120). And this time, too, the exhibition was naturally criticized, not in the British press, which praised it, but in the Danish. The exhibition was criticized for being too retrospective. "An atmospheric funeral in London for everything that took Denmark to the top of the international world of design," wrote Svend Erik Møller in the newspaper Politiken. It was the exhibition's content that was criticized; even Politiken acclaimed Finn Juhl's design.

The driving force behind the Society's large-scale exhibitions during the time was its chairman, Anders Hostrup-Pedersen, who was the director of the Georg Jensen silversmithy, one of the few Danish decorative arts companies which had a true international reputation and had had one for many years. Before the Second World War, the company had its own outlets in London, Paris, Berlin, Brussels, Geneva, Barcelona, Stockholm, St. Thomas, Buenos Aires, and New York, everywhere on the most distinguished shopping streets. The store on Fifth Avenue in New York belonged not to George Jen-

One of the exhibition interiors from the Georg Jensen silversmithy anniversary exhibition at the Museum of Decorative Art in 1954. Unfortunately, the colors that give the right impression of the light, elegant arrangement are lacking. See also page 111.

sen, however, but to Frederik Lunning, the founder of the Lunning Prize for Scandinavian designers.

Anders Hostrup-Pedersen, who was trained as a engineer before becoming the director of the Georg Jensen silversmithy in 1937, was forced to witness the company's decline during the war, but after these difficult years he led it to a new period of expansion. The smithy's strength had always lain in its high artistic quality, first through the pioneering contribution of Georg Jensen, and then through that of other excellent designers such as Johan Rohde, Harald Nielsen, and Gundorph Albertus. Anders Hostrup-Pedersen maintained this standard of high quality, since he employed a new generation of designers: Henning Koppel, Søren Georg Jensen (the old silversmith's son), Sigvard Bernadotte, Magnus Stephensen, Nanna and Jørgen Ditzel, Torun Bülow-Hübe, and many others.

In 1954, the silversmithy celebrated its fiftieth anniversary, and the occasion was marked by a large-scale exhibition at the Museum of Decorative Art arranged by Finn Juhl (page 111). A smaller version of this exhibition, one of Finn Juhl's finest, was later shown in the United States under the name of "50 Years of Danish Silver" (page 115).

The collaboration between Anders Hostrup-Pedersen and Finn Juhl developed into a life-long friendship. They had the same outlook on art and on arts and crafts, and Hostrup-Pedersen often asked Juhl's opinion on artistic matters. In addition, they were both cosmopolitans and had a bit of the same aristocratic view of life. Those who did not know Anders Hostrup-Pedersen might get the impression that he was something of a playboy, a pleasure-seeker, who because of his economic independence (he was one of the owners of the smithy) was able to travel around the world and loaf. He was

The Georg Jensen store in Toronto, Canada, which Finn Juhl designed in 1956. After the anniversary exhibition in 1954, he became a kind of "court architect" for the silversmithy, commissioned to design both exhibitions and store interiors in the United States, Britain, and Canada.

A living room in the new Danish ambassador's residence in Washington, D.C., with furnishings designed by Finn Juhl in 1960.

PRESSEHUSET

a gourmet and connoisseur of good wines (a member of the *confrères des vins* in Beaune and an honorary citizen of the city), and he even wrote a cookbook. But he was anything but a playboy. On the contrary: he was dynamic and full of initiative and, through unflagging work as chairman of the Danish Society of Arts and Crafts, was largely responsible for creating an international reputation for Danish arts and crafts, and with it, a considerable export market for them in the 1960s.

After the anniversary exhibition, Finn Juhl became Georg Jensen's official architect, defining the company's public image. He had already modernized Frederik Lunning's store on Fifth Avenue in 1952, and now he was also to modernize the Georg Jensen store on New Bond Street in London (together with the British architect Trevor Danatt). It was 1957, and the following year he designed the new Georg Jensen store in Toronto, Canada, and a couple of years later a new store in West Chester, Pennsylvania. He also designed a private summer house for Anders Hostrup-Pedersen in Raageleje, north of Copenhagen (page 104).

One commission that Finn Juhl accepted with great pleasure but some reservation was furnishing the Danish ambassador's residence in Washington, D.C. The embassy and adjoining residence had been designed by his old mentor, Vilhelm Lauritzen. Was the egg now to start teaching the hen? But their collaboration went smoothly, and to their mutual satisfaction. The embassy was inaugurated in 1960 during the royal couple's visit, when the large exhibition at the Metropolitan Museum of Art in New York was also opened.

The embassy was furnished almost entirely with Finn Juhl's own furniture. As is always the case when the state is involved, the funds available were limited. And since furnishing is the last phase in the construction process, that was naturally where money had to be saved. Finn Juhl did not get everything the way he wanted it. He had, for example, decided that the deck chairs on the terrace were to be Kaare Klint's teak deck chairs, but to cut costs, plastic chairs were chosen instead. Finn Juhl would not stand for it and paid for the chairs out of his own pocket!

It is inconceivable that Finn Juhl was able to carry out all the commissions he was given in the 1950s: the Trusteeship Council Chamber at the United Nations; the projects for SAS, which involved so much traveling; the major exhibitions in Switzerland, Italy, and the United States; the Georg Jensen anniversary exhibition; the museum room in Trondheim; the movie theater in Vangede; at the same time, designing a number of new types of furniture for Bovirke, France & Søn, and several other furniture manufacturers. Even though he naturally had a good staff, he always made his personal mark on all the projects, big and small. The many drawings that he left show that all projects were carefully worked out and were largely designed by Finn Juhl himself.

But in the 1960s, the flow of commissions began to ebb out. The large design office in Sølvgade, which had been needed for the work for SAS, was closed, and his office was moved to his home on Kratvænget. The last times he took part in the Copenhagen Cabinetmakers' Guild exhibitions were in 1961 and 1965. The furniture that he exhibited in 1961 gave rise to considerable debate (page 46), and it was never produced. Throughout the 1960s, he made a large num-

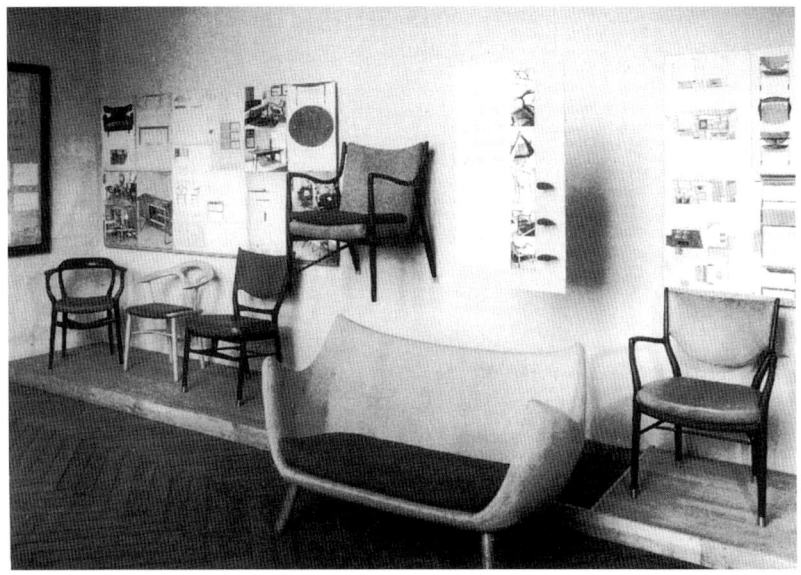

STRÜWING

Finn Juhl was invited at a twenty-year interval to exhibit his work at Charlottenborg, for the first time in 1950, then in 1970. The picture is from the exhibition in 1950.

ber of furniture designs for Bovirke, France & Søn, Fritz Hansens Eft., and Poul Cadovius, but very few of them were produced.

Even though the drawings, which are now found at Copenhagen's Museum of Decorative Art, include many fine furniture designs, there is no doubt that he had a difficult time renewing himself. Worst of all, he himself was able to see that his early furniture was the best he had created. The last furniture he designed was for Poul Cadovius in 1974, and it was never produced either.

His only major furnishing projects in the 1960s were the restaurant at the Hotel Richmond (page 88) and remodeling the Wilhelm Hansens Musikforlag store on Gothersgade (page 86).

At the end of the 1960s, he had some problems with his health, but the large exhibition in 1968 at the Victoria & Albert Museum in London, in Glasgow, and in Manchester showed that he was still a master at carrying out a large and complicated project in an elegant and convincing way. The very next year, the Danish Society of Arts and Crafts commissioned him to design a new exhibition. The Salle d'Exposition des Métiers d'Art in Brussels was to be the site of a larger exhibition, with the Society, the Federation of Danish Industries, the Danish Furniture Manufacturers' Association, and other organizations participating. Finn Juhl was commissioned to design the arts and crafts section. It was no easy task, since the room provided was not particularly suitable, and since a number of accidents occurred during the preparations which made it impossible to start setting up the exhibition until quite late. In addition, certain deliveries and the catalogue were delayed.

Nonetheless, the exhibition was completed on time. Afterwards, the director of the Society, Bent Salicath, wrote to Finn Juhl and thanked him for his contribution: "And there the exhibition was. Without any sign of the difficulties that had preceded it. Melodious in its composition, and with a central theme maintained that completely changed the character of the room and gave it a wholly new expression. There might be details with a view to the objects chosen that could perhaps have been carried out even better if there had been time, but these were insignificant details because the overall impression and accentuation provided by the placement of the objects gave a rhythm and melody to the tone set. Personally, I would

Finn Juhl photographed at his retrospective at Charlottenborg in 1970.

POLITIKENS PRESSEFOTO

Finn Juhl being awarded a diploma as Honorary Royal Designer for Industry by the president of the Royal Society of Arts, Sir Peter Masefield, on November 1, 1978.

UNITED PRESS

not have been afraid to move this exhibition to a Triennial, since it gave a distinctive, uniform expression which held a standard. This is precisely where the difference between being a skilled decorator and being an artist lies, even though the commission is presumably the same."[6]

The exhibition in Brussels was Finn Juhl's last for the Society, but by then he had arranged exhibitions of applied arts in some sixty places abroad. It was for all intents and purposes his last work of any kind. A score of years ensued with practically no commissions.

Finn Juhl did, however, organize one more exhibition, his own retrospective at the Museum of Decorative Art in 1982. It must have been a great source of satisfaction for him that precisely this museum, which had been so long in recognizing his contribution to furniture design, wanted to celebrate his 70th birthday. In the exhibition catalogue the museum's director, Erik Lassen, admitted "with shame" that he himself had not been able to view Finn Juhl's furniture objectively at a time when it was new and different. He admitted that at a party he had once loudly proclaimed that the Danish Museum of Decorative Art could note with satisfaction that it was the only museum of applied art in the world where Finn Juhl's furniture was not to be found!

The museum's acquisition records indeed show that the museum did not purchase its first two pieces of furniture by Finn Juhl until 1952.

The exhibition was an admirable success and was covered widely in the press, where Finn Juhl was acclaimed as one of the great coryphaei of Danish applied art.

Official recognition was not lacking during these years, either. He was granted a life-long pension in the state budget in 1971, and in 1984 he was made a Knight of the Order of the Dannebrog. He had been awarded a special foreign distinction in 1978, when the Royal Society of Arts in London made him an Honorary Royal Designer for Industry (HonRDI), an honor which few Danish designers have been given. One could say that it came twenty years too late, but late is, as we know, better than never.

In the following, a number of Finn Juhl's most important creations will be considered more closely.

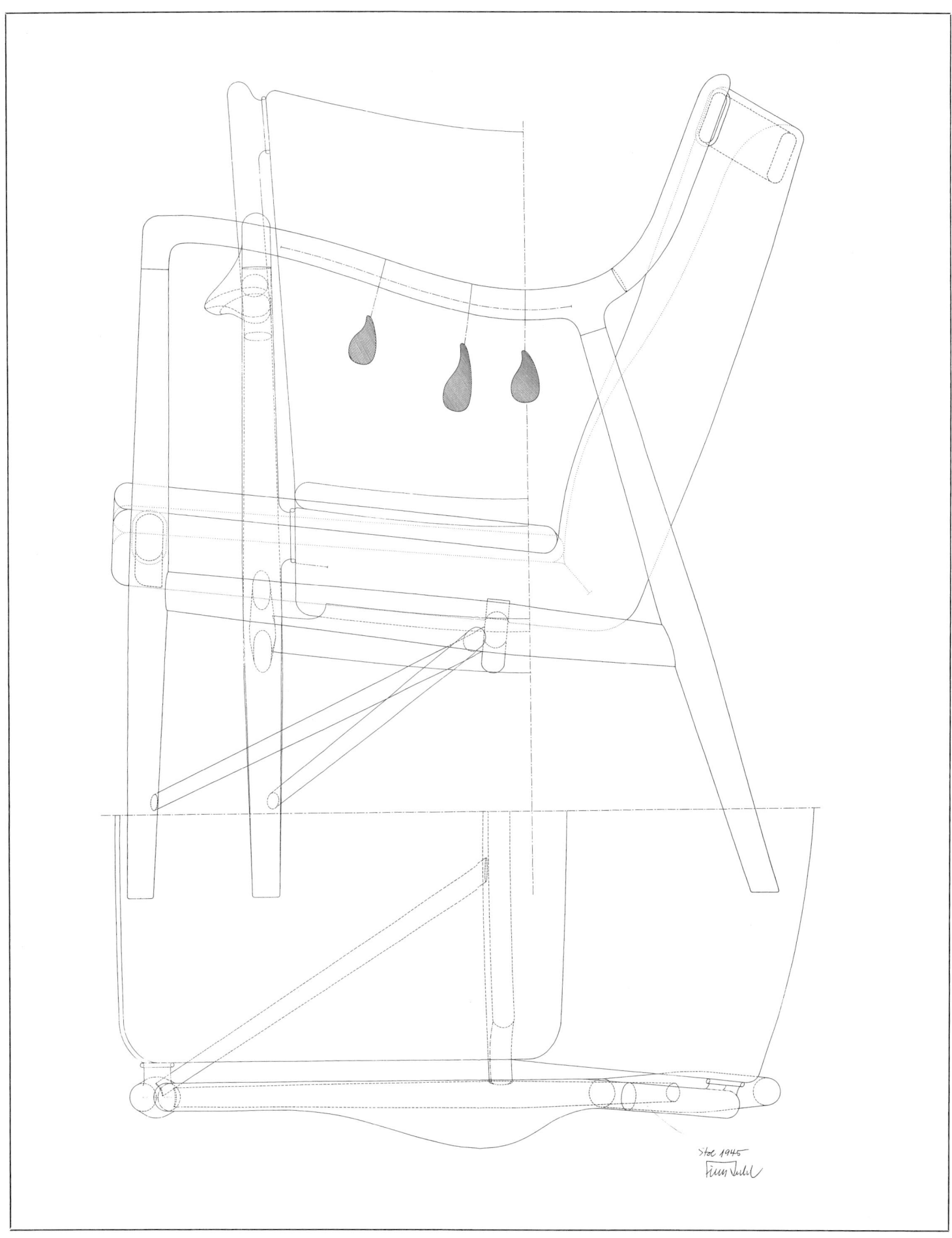

FURNITURE

It may seem inconceivable today that Finn Juhl's furniture was considered highly controversial when it was shown in the 1940s at the Cabinetmakers' Guild exhibitions at the Museum of Decorative Art. In order to understand this, it is necessary to realize that times were different – even in the field of furniture. The furniture of the day was first and foremost conservative, both that sold in furniture stores and the more select handcrafted furniture. It was the age of traditional furniture suites. Practical individual pieces of furniture which could be combined as one liked were almost nonexistent. People bought (usually on credit) "a living room," "a dining room," or "a bedroom suite," and they were in a specific (more or less undefinable) style. There were modified styles that were supposed to be renaissance, baroque, rococo, or "English." If one wanted something more modern, there was the lumpy "Chesterfield furniture." Those who wanted something ultramodern could choose the steel furniture of the 1930s.

There was practically no furniture industry that experimented with new forms and production methods. Only the old chair manufacturer, Fritz Hansens Eftf., was developing into a modern furniture manufacturer. It started producing steel furniture and furniture made of steam-bent wood using Thonet's method. But it was a loner that did not change the profile of a furniture industry that consisted more or less of large joineries.

Reform was inevitable, and it came first and foremost from Kaare Klint. At his initiative, a department of furniture design was founded in 1924 at the Royal Academy of Fine Arts' School of Architecture that was to prove of considerable importance for the development of Danish furniture design. Kaare Klint's school, as it was called with good reason, influenced a whole generation of architects, furniture designers, and joiners. The special feature of Klint's teaching was that he introduced a stringent work method based on studies of function. It was the interplay between the dimensions of the human body, the function of furniture, and a good knowledge of wood as a material that became the basis for furniture design. Logic, often using a mathematical system of measures, and a constructive way of thinking were the foundation for Klint's philosophy of furniture. He claimed that only by analysing the prerequisites for a piece of furniture was it possible to reach a sensible design. "On the basis of these dry facts, one can learn to build up a piece of furniture; anyone can then give it the changing, artistic form that suits him and the times," he wrote in 1930 in an article in Arkitekten on the goals and methods of his school.

Klint was disdainful of the view that his school taught aesthetics, but it was naturally inevitable that the pieces of furniture he himself designed served as textbook examples. They were, after all, the result

Work drawing on a scale of 1:1 for the "45 Chair," here reproduced on a scale of 1:5.

MAARBJERG

of his methods. But there was not much innovation involved. In reality, Kaare Klint was highly conservative. The forms of his own furniture were based on English furniture types from the 18th century, especially Chippendale. He removed all ornamentation and refined them so that only their basic forms remained. As a result, they met the day's demand for simplicity. Even his most untraditional types of furniture were based on models. The safari chair (1933), which became so popular, was modeled on the British officer's camp chair from colonial times. The deck chair (designed the same year) was a refinement of the deck chairs found on the large Atlantic liners. The church chair (1936) was inspired by the spindlebacked chairs with rush-plaited seat that are found in innumerable Catholic churches in the Mediterranean.

Kaare Klint considered it right in principle to build furniture on the experiences of earlier generations as far as the furniture's construction, joinings, and dimensioning of the wood were concerned. He considered such accumulated results as public domain to be built upon. Digressions often led only to deterioration. He com-

MAARBJERG

Interiors from Niels Vodder's stand at the Cabinetmakers' Guild exhibitions in 1940 (above) and 1941 (below).
During this period, Finn Juhl worked especially with overstuffed furniture. It is obvious that he was highly influenced by contemporary sculpture.
He himself emphasized this by exhibiting his furniture together with works of art of the day, in 1940 a wooden sculpture, and in 1941 a plaster relief by Sigurjón Ólafsson. Opposite page: Above, Kaare Klint's famous "red chair", which he designed for the Museum of Decorative Art's lecture hall in 1927. It was upholstered with red Niger leather, which gave it's name. The construction of the chair is completely traditional. Below is a chair designed by Finn Juhl for Niels Vodder in 1951. The seat and back are entirely separate from the finely formed bearing frame.

pletely rejected the Bauhaus school's attempts to achieve modern furniture design by wiping the slate clean and starting from the beginning, as if furniture had never been designed before.

Kaare Klint's furniture was highly admired, and it is no exaggeration to say that it formed a school. Even furniture designers who had never attended his classes worked with his methods and in his style. This could be seen at the Cabinetmakers' Guild exhibitions precisely during the period when Finn Juhl began to design furniture. He had not attended Klint's school, and consequently did not feel bound by its norms. He stood out with his work with freer design, which contrasted with the more stringent geometrically-determined Klint style.

The Cabinetmakers' Guild exhibitions
During the first years Finn Juhl showed his work at the Cabinetmakers' Guild exhibitions, he was especially preoccupied by overstuffed chairs and sofas with highly sculptural forms. "Finn Juhl's chairs for the cabinetmaker Niels Vodder are very strangely formed; they mostly resemble tired walruses," said a review in Arkitekten. The question of the extent to which Finn Juhl was inspired by contemporary art in his furniture design will be taken up later, but there is no doubt about it in this first furniture. At the exhibition in 1940, he himself emphasized this influence by adorning the stand with an abstract wooden sculpture by Erik Thommesen. The kinship between it and the furniture is highly conspicuous.

Finn Juhl was a great admirer of Erik Thommesen's art, and throughout the years that he took part in the Cabinetmakers' Guild exhibitions he often had a wooden sculpture by Thommesen at his stand. When he furnished the museum room in Trondheim, a large sculpture by Thommesen was an important part of its design (page 78). He had several of Thommesen's sculptures in his own home on Kratvænget.

Overstuffed furniture was, however, a constructively unclear type that in the long run was unable to satisfy Finn Juhl. Already at the exhibition in 1941, he showed the armchair that was to be his most characteristic type of furniture. The upholstered part, consisting of seat and back in one piece, is supported by a visible wooden construction. He refined this type with virtuosity in the years that followed. It culminated as early as 1945 in his most harmonious and painstakingly conceived chair, the "45 chair," but many variations appeared in the following years.

This principle, separating the seat and back from the bearing wooden frame, was in fact one thing that broke with traditional furniture construction. Finn Juhl used it in most of his furniture, not only in easy chairs, but also in other types of chairs.

A customary chair is constructed either with the legs, backrest, and arms (if any), mortised down into the seat, for example as in the well-known Windsor chair, or else with the legs, backrest, and arms (if any), joined by a frame so that legs, back, and seat form a unit. This construction can be seen, for example, in Kaare Klint's famous "red chair."

The principle of separating the bearing frame from the seat and back was naturally not something that came to Finn Juhl as a revelation. It was a principle that had long been under development. As far back as 1917, the Dutchman G.T. Rietveld had designed the famous "red and blue chair" in which all constructive parts were separate. It was probably conceived more as an artistic manifestation than as an attempt to design a utilitarian piece of furniture, but it is quite an interesting analysis of the chair as a concept. Elements from this construction – in modified form – are found in experimental furniture right to the present day. At Bauhaus, Marcel Breuer, who headed the school's furniture workshop, also worked with analyzing elements of the chair, and designed several types of furniture in which the seat and bearing frame were clearly separated. This was true of the steel tube chairs that were devised during the period, where the principle was natural. Denmark also had several furniture designers who tried their hand at it, for example Tove and Edvard Kindt-Larsen in their "fireside chair" from 1940.

But Finn Juhl worked consistently with this construction, creating a number of distinctive types of furniture on this basis. His ability to design elegant, supple forms was developed by working with the various parts of the wooden frame. He reached a culmination in 1949 with his "Chieftain Chair."

It was not only in chairs that Finn Juhl refined this principle, but also in tables, where he freed the table top from the frame so that it almost seemed to hover, giving the tables an incomparable lightness.

Finn Juhl's treatment of wood is almost a chapter in itself. Wood is, after all, a wonderful material which permits itself to be shaped and which is strong and pliant when it is used in conformity with its nature. Two pieces of wood can be joined almost invisibly, and the joints can be so strong that if the wood breaks under too heavy a load, the break often occurs outside the joint. Throughout the centuries, the joiner's craft has developed rules for how "correct" joints should be made. In the beginning, Finn Juhl was often accused of subjecting wood to more than was good for it in order to achieve supple, sculptural forms, and it was felt that his joints were not made correctly. This is where his work with the skilled cabinetmaker Niels Vodder proved valuable, since Vodder was able to execute difficult, untraditional joints so that they held, despite predictions to the contrary.

The choice of the correct type of wood, which corresponded to the furniture's character, was decisive for Finn Juhl. When he began to design furniture, mahogany was the only one for fine furniture. Those who could not afford mahogany used beech that was given a mahogany stain. With a few exceptions, Kaare Klint always used mahogany, and preferably Cuban mahogany. When this fine type of wood was no longer available because of over-exploitation, he turned to other types of mahogany and to oak. He used beech for his church chair. Finn Juhl, on the contrary, used other fine types of wood, such as maple, cherry wood, Oregon pine, cedar, walnut, palisander, and especially teak. He was evidently the first designer to use this wood for indoor furniture on a large scale. Normally it was used outside, because of its large plant gum content. What appealed to Finn Juhl was that it did not need any protective varnish. It only needed a bit of oil to keep its lovely glow.

Finn Juhl was also one of the first to bring color to furniture, since he painted certain fields and panels in hues that harmonized with the interior and suited the type of wood used.

Until the end of the 1940s, Finn Juhl had designed furniture exclusively for Niels Vodder, and this had given him great freedom to ex-

Rietveld's famous "red and blue chair" designed in 1917. The chair is an analysis of the chair as a concept, but is probably intended to be more a three-dimensional cubistic "painting" than a utilitarian piece of furniture. The frame is black and yellow, the seat blue, and the back-rest red.

Furniture at the Cabinetmakers' Guild exhibition in 1944 made by Niels Vodder: "Hot table," wall cupboard, and armchair. The armchair is also shown on page 34. The cupboard has sliding doors with painted panels.

MAARBJERG

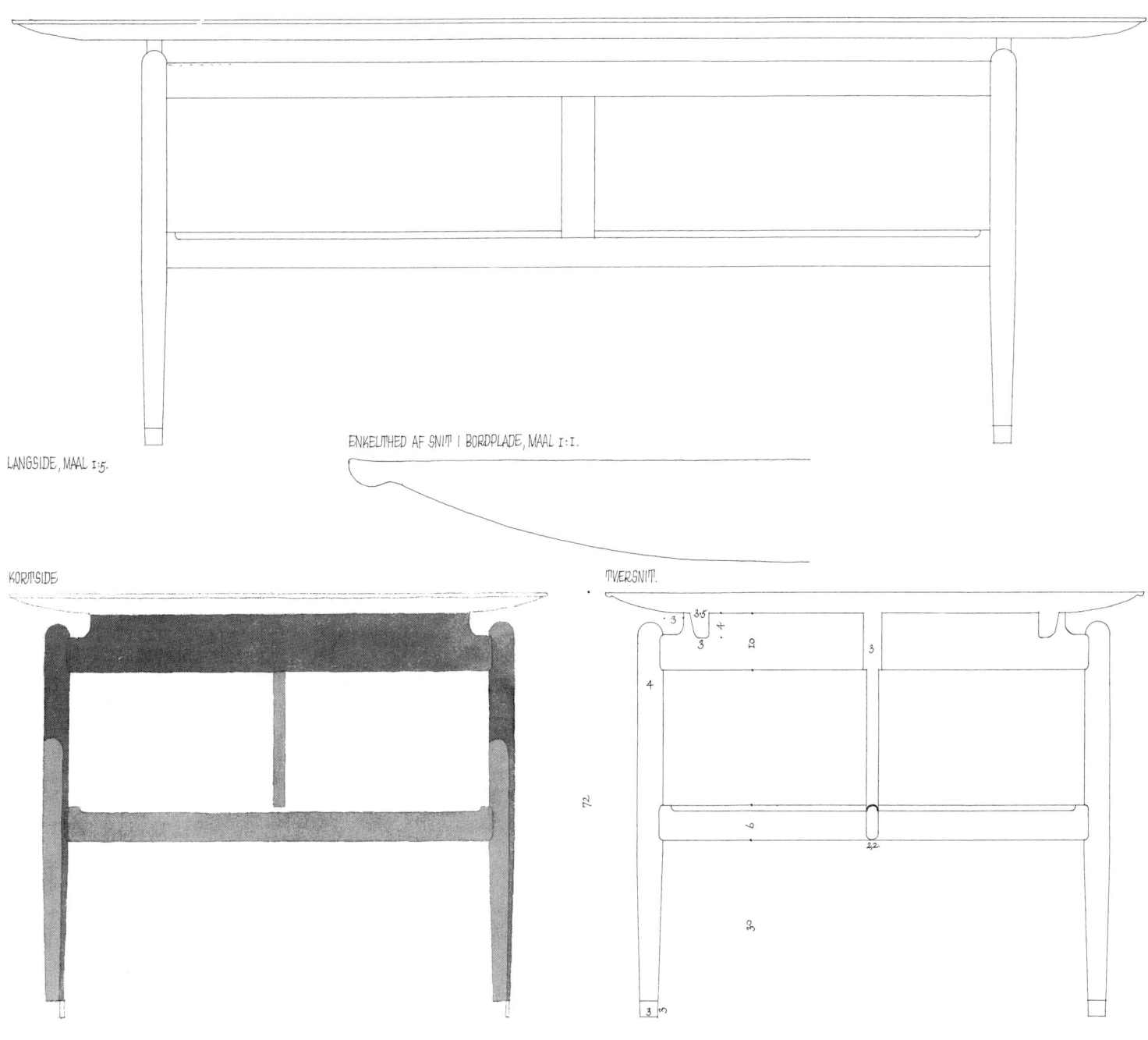

Work table designed in 1945 and exhibited the same year at the Cabinetmakers' Guild exhibition, made by Niels Vodder. Here Finn Juhl worked with liberating the table top visually from the supporting frame. It is probably one of Finn Juhl's loveliest tables, and he also used it when he furnished the room at the museum in Trondheim. See page 79.

periment with forms and constructions. From the beginning of the 1950s, the furniture industry entered the picture, however, and conditions here were tougher.

The Danish furniture industry was waking up. It realized that it had to go in for a more modern style of furniture. In 1942, the organization of furniture dealers had held a major exhibition at the Forum exhibition hall under the title of *Tidens Møbler* (Furniture of the Day). It was given rough treatment by the critics. "Ugly Furniture at Forum," wrote Ole Wanscher, later professor of furniture design at the Academy, in his review in the Danish Society of Arts and Crafts' periodical . The exhibition sparked off a lively debate. What was especially noted by critics was that the furniture industry did not produce furniture that ordinary people needed to furnish the small apartments that completely dominated public housing. It is obvious that there was a tremendous need for light, practical furniture and not for whole suites when we consider that almost half (46.8%) of all apartments in Copenhagen in 1950 had only two rooms and that nearly a quarter (23.6%) had only three.

In 1946, Danish furniture manufacturers followed the cabinetmakers' example and proclaimed a competition for furniture for the exhibition that was to take place the following year. The furniture industry's sharpest critic, Ole Wanscher, was on the jury. Many of the architects who took part had designed for cabinetmakers, including Finn Juhl, whose designs were among those awarded prizes. The criticism of the exhibition's furniture was more subdued this time, but not much of the furniture that was awarded prizes was produced, not even Finn Juhl's.

Furniture manufacturers considered his creations to be very special and difficult to produce in large series, and not without reason. "Finn Juhl's furniture is luxurious and upon occasion it is thus seen as an expression of arrogant aestheticism that conflicts with the rational simplicity that modern furniture design is otherwise based upon. He is probably not always blameless himself in this respect, and he wishes to challenge mathematical logic and also sometimes production requirements," wrote Bent Salicath in a review of the exhibition in the Danish Society of Arts and Crafts' periodical.[7]

Baker Furniture
It was an American furniture company, and not a Danish one, that first tackled Finn Juhl's furniture. In November 1948, Edgar Kauf-

OLE WOLDBYE

THE NEW YORK TIMES

The little armchair with the sculpturally contoured frame was designed for the Cabinetmakers' Guild exhibition in 1944 and made of palisander by Niels Vodder. Only 12 copies were produced of the chair, which must be considered one of his masterpieces.

This spread: The "45 Chair," designed for the Cabinetmakers' Guild exhibition in 1945 and made by Niels Vodder, is another one of Finn Juhl's masterpieces. In it he refined the type of easy chair that he had been working with for a number of years: a chair where the seat and back are liberated in a logical way from the wooden bearing frame.

SCHNAKENBURG & BRAHL

MAARBJERG

mann, Jr., had presented Finn Juhl in the United States in an article in the respected periodical Interiors with the title "Finn Juhl of Copenhagen." It was read by Hollis S. Baker, president of the large American furniture company Baker Furniture, Inc. of Grand Rapids, Michigan. The photographs of Finn Juhl's furniture which accompanied the article appealed to him and he decided that he could use this furniture to introduce a modern line in Baker Furniture's production, which had so far especially comprised reproductions. In June 1950, he visited Finn Juhl at his design office in Copenhagen's Nyhavn and proposed that they collaborate. Finn Juhl was initially sceptical about whether an American company would be able to live up to the quality that he wanted for his furniture, and which Niels Vodder was able to deliver. Mr. Baker invited Finn Juhl to visit him in Grand Rapids that coming autumn. When he saw Baker Furniture's production, his scepticism was overcome, and an agreement was made under which Baker Furniture was to manufacture and sell some of the furniture that was already being produced by Niels Vodder (and sold in Denmark), and have new models designed that were especially suited to the American market. One stipulation of the agreement was that the new furniture, which was to be sold under the name of Baker Modern, should be ready in time for the big furniture fair in Grand Rapids the following year. The meeting at which the contract was signed took place in September 1950, and the fair was to open in June 1951, so a typically American schedule had to be met.

The contract also stipulated that Finn Juhl would design a showroom for Baker to present the new furniture range in conjunction with the fair. Luckily, drawings could be flown back and forth, and both furniture and showroom were ready on time. When the models were presented, Baker Furniture even emphasized that large series of furniture were ready, and not just the pieces shown at the exhibition: deliveries could be made right after the fair. American efficiency!

All in all, Baker Furniture manufactured 24 furniture models designed by Finn Juhl.

This spread: Finn Juhl designed a number of pieces of furniture for the Cabinetmakers' Guild exhibition in 1948 for a "workroom for an art collector." Like many of his entries throughout the years, it was made by Niels Vodder for the exhibition and awarded a prize. There were, however, two rooms, one with a fireplace, easy chairs, and "stool table," and a workroom with a work table, armchairs, sofa bench, and sofa table. The "fireplace chairs," which could be joined, were made of maple and Cuban mahogany with woolen upholstery and a cowhide neck rest. Brass trays for whisky glasses were set into the armrests. The chairs were never manufactured.

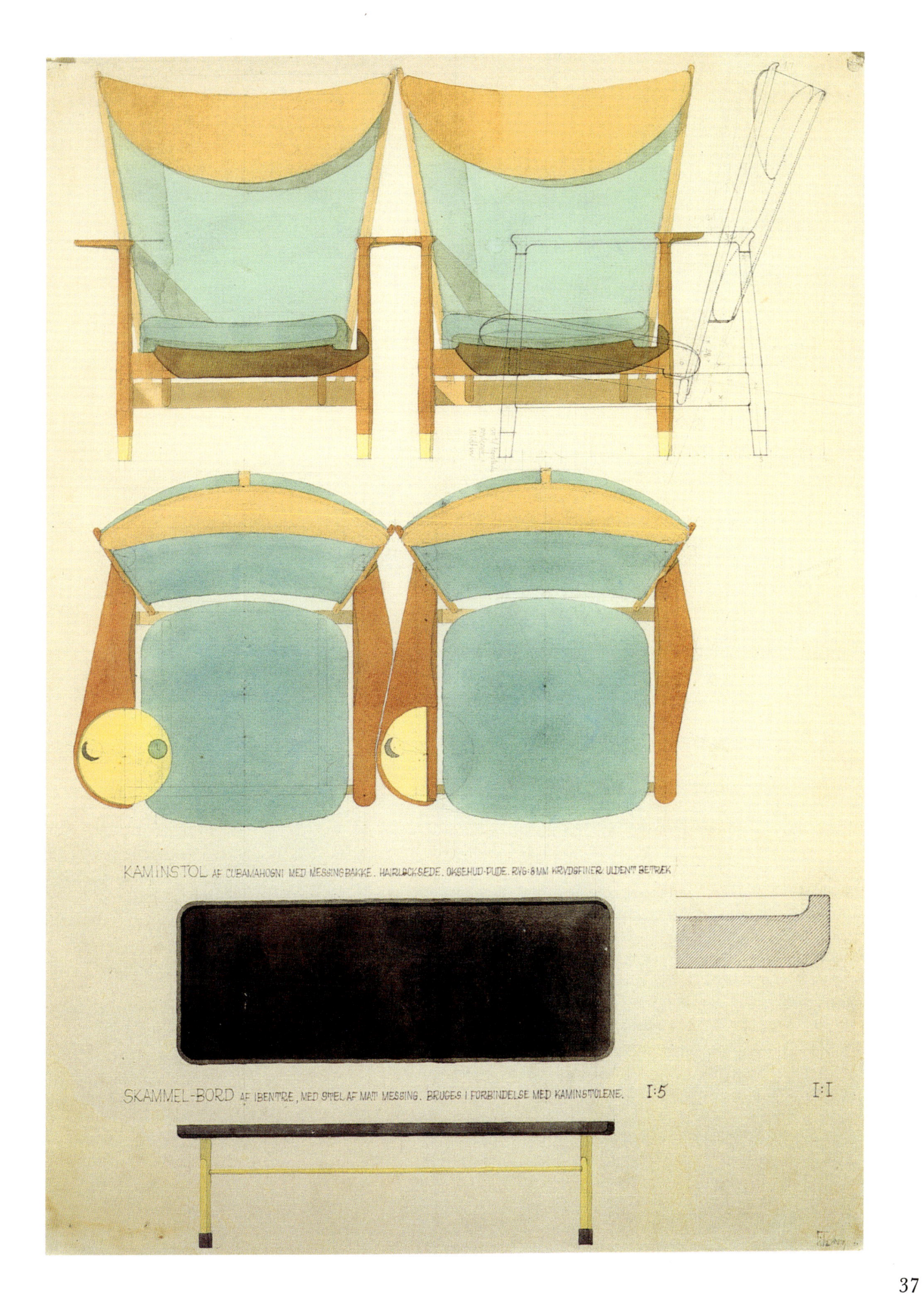

KAMINSTOL AF CUBAMAHOGNI MED MESSINGBAKKE. HAIRLOCKSÆDE. OKSEHUD-PUDE. RYG: 8 MM KRYDSFINER/ ULDENT BETRÆK

SKAMMEL-BORD AF IBENTRÆ, MED STEL AF MAT MESSING. BRUGES I FORBINDELSE MED KAMINSTOLENE.   1:5   1:1

This spread: Finn Juhl designed the elegant sofa bench and armchair with the same construction for the "workroom for an art collector" at the Cabinetmakers' Guild exhibition in 1948. For the exhibition, they were made of maple and Cuban mahogany and upholstered with cowhide. The sofa table was also made of mahogany and maple. There was a detachable tray with a glass plate under the hinged leaves. The armchairs were later manufactured by Baker Furniture, Inc. in the United States in other types of wood.

OLE WOLDBYE

Bovirke
The first Danish furniture manufacturer who believed that Finn Juhl could design furniture that could be produced industrially was Poul Lund. He was actually a furniture salesman, head of the large Bovirke furniture store in Frederiksberg, in Greater Copenhagen. He had contacted Finn Juhl back in 1947 to sound out the possibility of collaboration, but their work together did not start until 1950. The first piece of furniture, a "fireside chair," did not see the light of day until 1952. This was at about the same time that the first furniture from Baker Furniture in the United States reached the stores, so the claim that Finn Juhl's furniture had to be accepted in the United States before it was produced industrially in Denmark is not correct. The chair was incidentally the first piece by Finn Juhl purchased by the Museum of Decorative Art in Copenhagen. At the time it cost $41.

Finn Juhl designed a number of good pieces for Bovirke, among other things a practical panel wall, and many of them were exported through Bovirke's special export company, BO-EX.

France & Søn
The next furniture manufacturer that contacted Finn Juhl was France & Daverkosen of Ørholm. It was actually a mattress company (Lama mattresses), but the English-born businessman C.W.F. France had gotten the good idea of making chair cushions if it was possible to have furniture designed that required loose cushions. He contacted several of the best furniture designers, since Mr. France was not only enterprising and imaginative, but also had a feel for quality. One of those he contacted was Finn Juhl, and the result was years of fruitful collaboration, especially after France started his own furniture company, France & Søn, in Hillerød.

Finn Juhl preferred teak and he believed that it was especially suited to industrially manufactured furniture because it did not require as much finishing. But one difficulty arose that seemingly made it impossible. Teak contains so much plant gum that the blades used to cut it are quickly dulled. This was not a big problem in the produc-

38

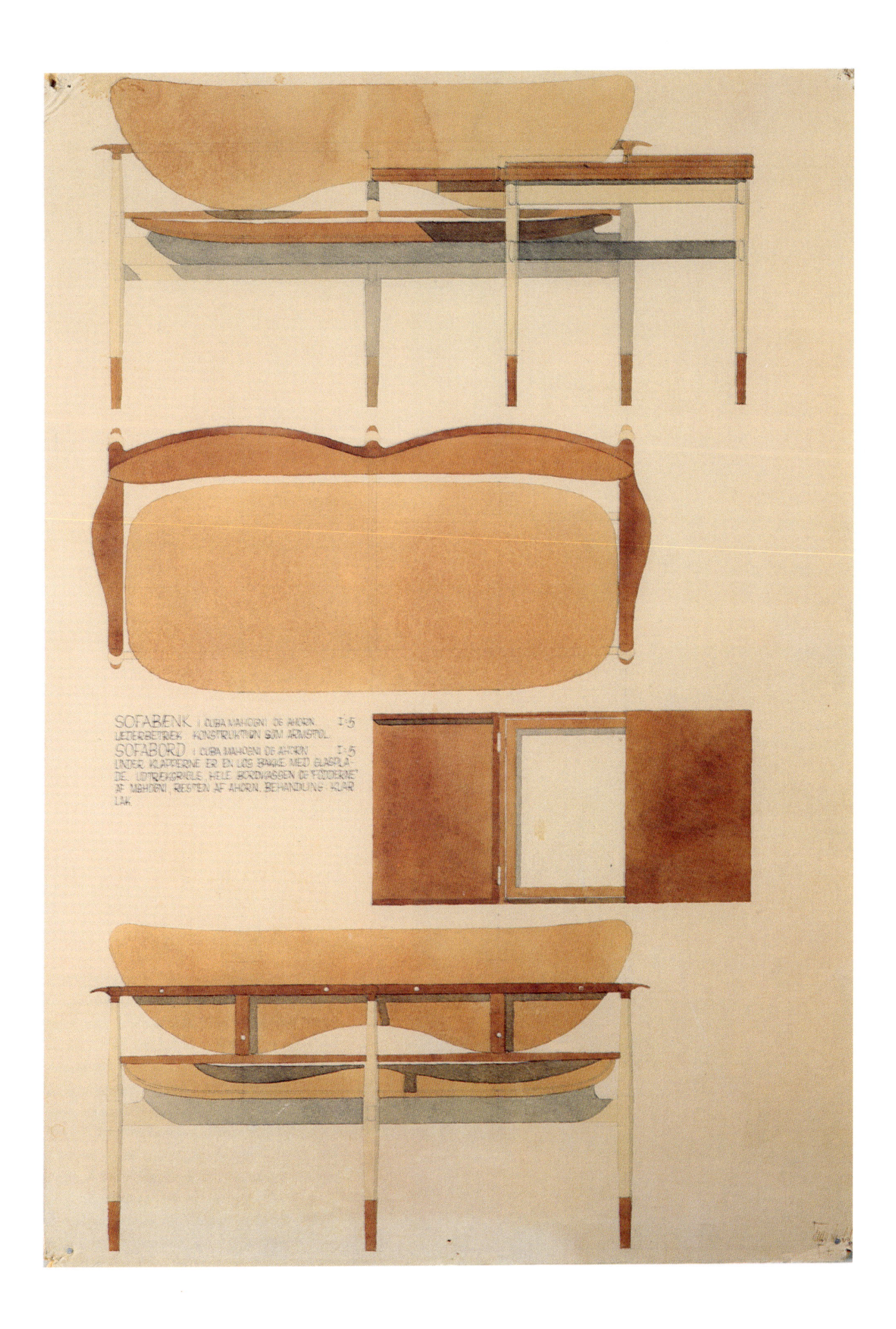

SOFABÆNK I CUBA MAHOGNI OG AHORN. 1:5
LÆDERBETRÆK. KONSTRUKTION SOM ARMSTOL.
SOFABORD I CUBA MAHOGNI OG AHORN. 1:5
UNDER KLAPPERNE ER EN LØS BAKKE MED GLASPLA-
DE. UDTRÆKSRILLE. HELE BORDVANGEN OG "FØDDERNE"
AF MAHOGNI, RESTEN AF AHORN. BEHANDLING: KLAR
LAK.

STRÜWING SCHNAKENBURG & BRAHL

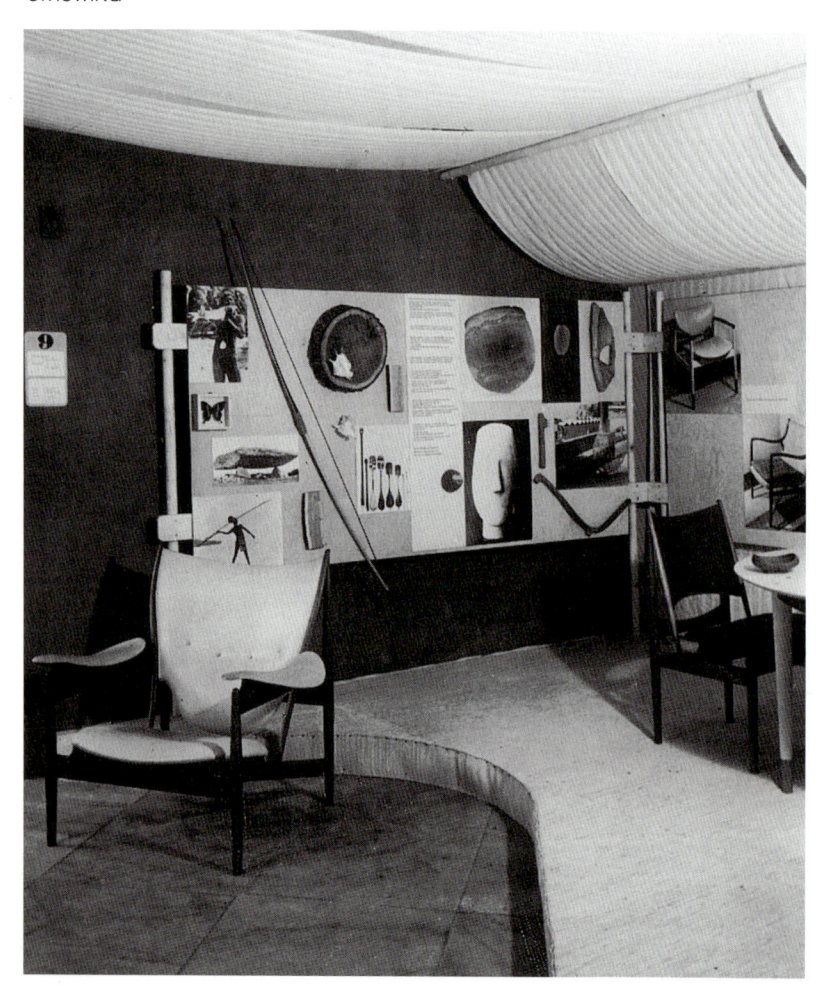

This spread: Finn Juhl designed the "Chieftain Chair," probably the most distinctive of all his furniture, for the Cabinetmakers' Guild exhibition in 1949. It did not get unmixed reviews from the critics at the time, but today most probably agree that it is one of his most important creations. At the exhibition, he showed that he had been inspired in the way he formed the chair's wooden frame by forms from the weapons and utilitarian objects of primitive peoples. It is not known whether the chair got its name in this way. Finn Juhl himself related that when the exhibition was opened, King Frederik IX had tried the chair. The designer was asked by a journalist if it should now be called "the king's chair," but he had considered it too pretentious and said, "You had better call it a chieftain's chair" – which the journalist did.

SCHNAKENBURG & BRAHL

tion of furniture by hand, but it was seemingly insurmountable when the wood had to be worked by machine. For example, a machine that rotates 400 times a second can profile thousands of components of oak or beech before the blades are dulled, but with teak, the cutter edges burn off when only a dozen pieces are put through the machine. But the ingenious Mr. France solved this problem. He had read that aluminum can be profiled using rotating tools with cutters made of a tungsten-carbide alloy with a very high melting point. It occurred to him that this method could also be used in the furniture industry – and he was right!

It was an advance for the furniture industry, but it meant that teak gradually became fashionable and that teak furniture harried the whole country and dominated exports as well, especially in the form of Finn Juhl plagiarisms. Unfortunately, it has always been true in decorative art that when an original item is a sales success, it is immediately copied, usually in a poorer quality or distorted version. At the time it was difficult to put a stop to this abuse, since the law on plagiarism was a law on artists. Only works of art were protected against unauthorized copying. But was a chair a work of art under law? That was the problem. The Danish Society of Arts and Crafts had to take several cases to court before it was decided that a chair, for example, could be an independent intellectual creation on a par with a work of art. The law that was later enacted on copyright made it easier to prosecute plagiarisms, but the problem still exists.

It was a serious problem for Finn Juhl since companies often stopped producing his furniture when it had been copied too blatantly. Things were so bad that Svend Erik Møller, in his review of the "Furniture of the Times" exhibition in 1952 wrote, "It is terribly depressing to see these watered down 'Finn Juhls' that have popped up recently. He is so personal and distinctive an artist that under no circumstances can one imitate his idiom."

France & Søn met with economic difficulties in 1966 and the company was bought the same year by Poul Cadovius's Royal System. All of the contracts and agreements with architects, including those with Finn Juhl, were included in the takeover. Royal Systems and France & Søn models were then marketed under the joint name of the Cado Collection. In 1968-69, Finn Juhl designed a new series of models for Cado, presented under the name of "Interline," but it was not a sales success. He designed several other models – the last in 1974 – but none of them was produced. Royal System closed in 1980.

Over the years the myth has grown up that Finn Juhl was rejected by Danish critics and that not until he had a made a name for himself in the United States did people begin to realize that his furniture was something special. This is not true. His earliest furniture was naturally met with criticism – which was often well founded – but the critics in fact became positive very quickly.

As early as 1945, Erik Herløv, later professor of industrial design at the Academy, wrote in a review in Arkitekten: "The most interesting thing at the exhibition was probably Finn Juhl's work, also because we clearly see a well resolved result of many years' experiments. He does not, unlike Wanscher, build upon a refinement of traditions, but has logically divided each project up into its functions and created forms for them himself. During the first years, these experiments seemed exaggerated, at times far-fetched, which

This spread: For the exhibition in 1949, Finn Juhl designed this settee, which was later called the "Double Chieftain Chair," and a sofa table with a hinged leaf made of Oregon pine and teak, with a mat-polished brass plate to hold hot things. The position of the legs and the form of the table top provide easy access to the settee.

STRÜWING

SOFABÆNK, 1:5, UDFØRES I IMBUJA OG MED OKSEHUD-BETRÆK. KONSTRUKTION SOM HVILESTOLENS.
KLAPBORD, 1:5, UDFØRES I TEAK OG OREGON-PINE MED BESLAG OG PLADE AF MATSLEBET MESSING.
PLADEFORM OG BENPLACERING GIVER NEM ADGANG TIL SOFAEN. "FRI" FORM DA INGEN FUNKTION STILLER BINDENDE KRAV.

YOSHIO HAYASHI

This spread: The "Egyptian Chair" was also designed for the exhibition in 1949 and made by Niels Vodder. Finn Juhl was clearly inspired by the refined Egyptian furniture that is known especially from the tomb of Tutankhamen. He later wrote in a feature article that it was at the Louvre that he first saw a well-preserved Egyptian chair with the characteristic side, a triangle formed by the vertical back legs, the frame that holds the diagonal back, and the horizontal rail between the front and back legs, a sturdy and simple construction: "I honestly admit that I have stolen the construction, just as I have stolen the right angle and the circle. It should also be admitted that I have been and am more captivated by the most simple and elegant furniture from Egypt than by other furniture of the past." (Politiken, Oct. 9, 1976). The picture on the left shows an Egyptian princess sitting on a chair of this type.

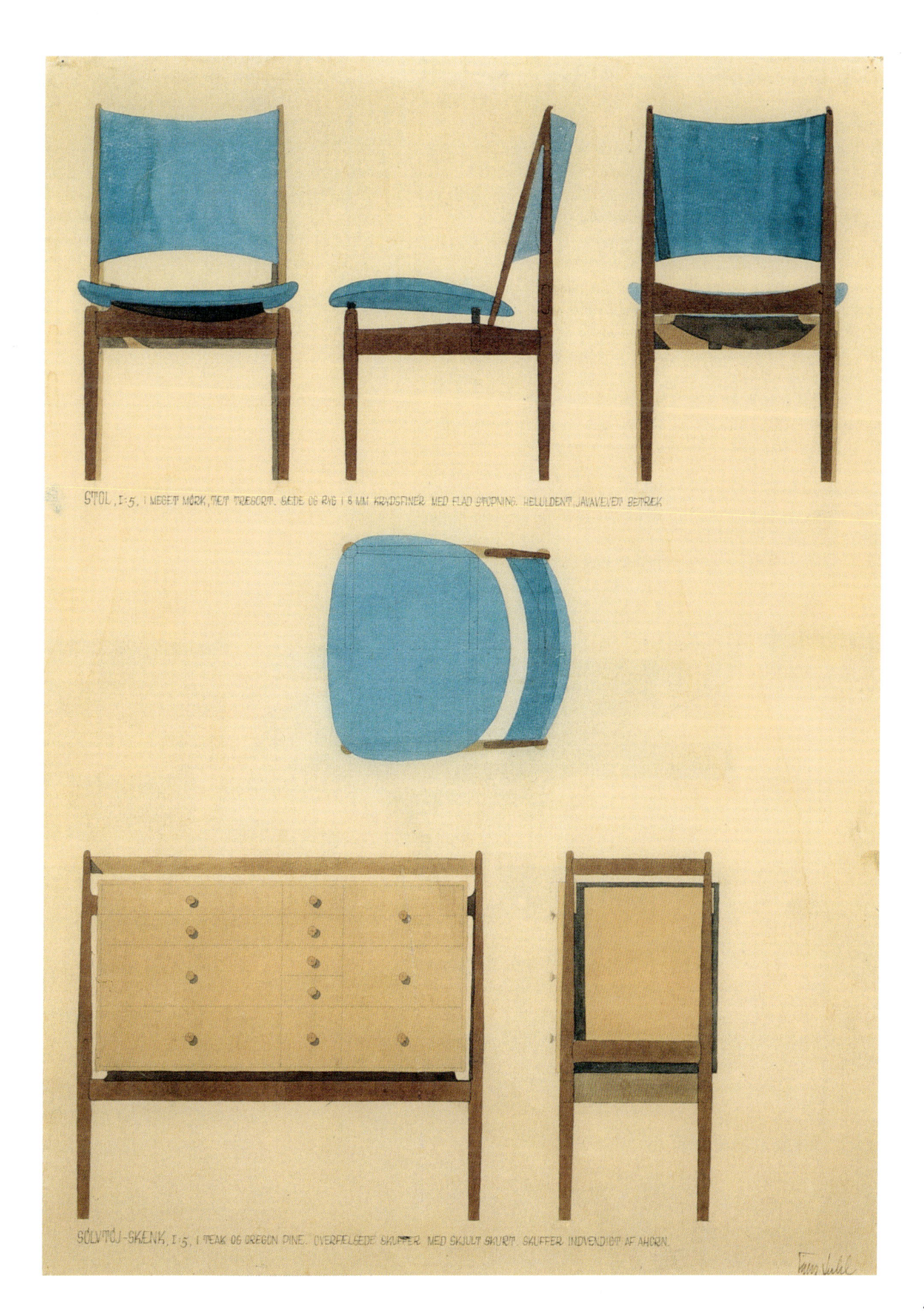

STOL, 1:5, I MEGET MØRK, TÆT TRÆSORT. SÆDE OG RYG I 8 MM KRYDSFINER MED FLAD STOPNING. HELULDENT, JAVAVÆVET BETRÆK

SØLVTØJ-SKÆNK, 1:5, I TEAK OG OREGON PINE. OVERFALSEDE SKUFFER MED SKJULT SKURT. SKUFFER INDVENDIGT AF AHORN.

makes it even more interesting now to observe the results which this man has achieved in his own way."[8]

In 1948, the highly critical Svend Erik Møller wrote in Nyt Tidskrift for Kunstindustri, "Finn Juhl has a wonderful innovative ability which is very much lacking elsewhere."[9]

If there nonetheless remains a picture of merciless criticism which kept a great talent down, it is probably due to a controversy much later, in 1962, at a time when Finn Juhl was widely recognized as an excellent designer. It was a major article entitled "Applied Art Gone Astray" which Arne Karlsen, later professor of furniture design at the School of Architecture in Århus, and the furniture designer Børge Mogensen wrote in Arkitekten. It had been preceded by a review of the Cabinetmakers' Guild exhibition in 1959 – also written by Karlsen and Mogensen – in the periodical Dansk Kunsthaandværk with the title "Illusion and Reality," where the two architects gave a critical review of the furniture exhibited and pointed out a large number of constructive and functional defects. (Finn Juhl's furniture was not among the pieces criticized.)[10]

The two adopted a more polemical tone in the new article. They based it on the Cabinetmakers' Guild exhibition in 1961, but believed they were justified in noting that Danish applied art as a whole was yielding to industry's demands for constant regeneration and an increasing number of salable forms.[11] Their main view was that "the work of developing types of objects, as was the ideal goal of both

This spread: The drawing shows the delegates' chair in the Trusteeship Council Chamber at the U.N. in its final form. See the sketches on pages 74-75. As shown in the picture, Baker Furniture, Inc., made the chair out of maple and teak in accordance with the drawing, while Niels Vodder made it completely of walnut for the U.N. and with upholstery in different colors than that shown here. The picture is from the Baker Furniture showroom, which Finn Juhl designed in 1951, where his furniture was presented. The sofa with the sculpturally contoured neck-rest was also made by Niels Vodder and shown at the Cabinetmakers' Guild exhibition the same year.

DALE ROOKS

47

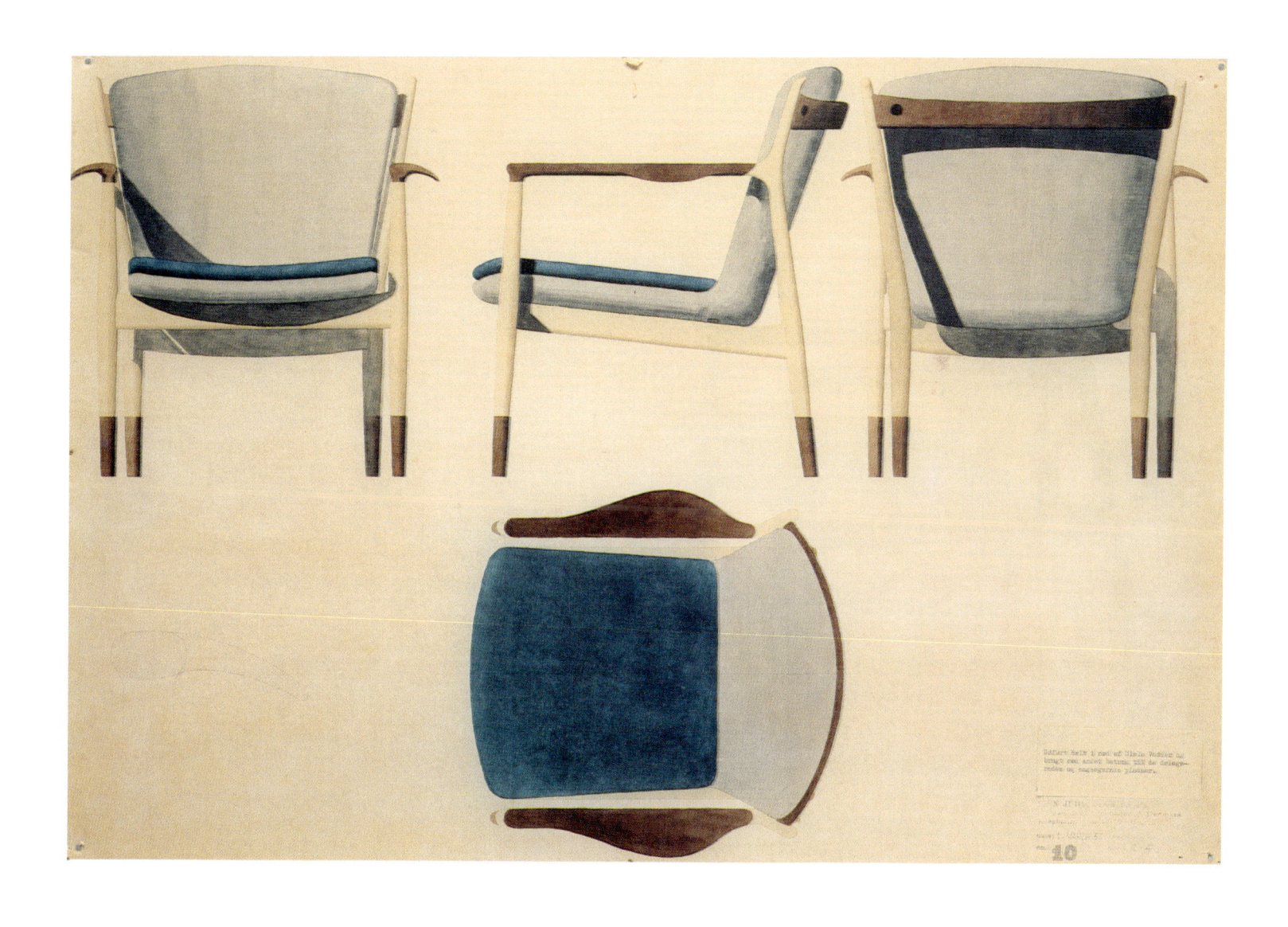

YOSHIO HAYASHI

YOSHIO HAYASHI

This spread: The armchair with the adjustable wicker back and its matching footrest were made by Niels Vodder for the Cabinetmakers' Guild exhibition in 1955. They were then also made by Baker Furniture, even though they were actually not very well suited to industrial manufacture. Niels Vodder made them completely out of teak. The armrests were made of laminated teak with visible maple dowels. In the United States, the chair was made of walnut.

49

the avant gardists and the Klint School, has disappeared completely, taken over by work with the external form of the individual piece of furniture. The individual designer's artistic self-assertion has been put uppermost through a unilateral worship of aesthetics."

They also criticized the fact that a higher standard of living brought with it a pandering to the elite, "as if all of life were a cocktail party, and as if the problems of furniture that are linked with the ceremonies of this kind of social life were the only ones that remain to be solved....Not until this year was the 'Beer glass for Denmark's Mr. Jones,' and everything it stands for, definitively replaced by a cocktail glass."

The article had many relevant views, but it was written in a dreary, sermonizing tone, and what was especially obnoxious was that it included attacks on several designers of applied art mentioned by name, among them Finn Juhl. They wrote the following, criticizing an interior by Finn Juhl at the Cabinetmakers' Guild exhibition – a bedroom with furniture that was decidedly experimental – and an old statement that he had made that furniture should be designed for living and not for museums: "Today Finn Juhl's furniture is found in all the celebrated museums of applied art the world over. Is he now rejecting the idiom he has used hitherto because he feels that the exaggeration of his artistic expression can only lead precisely straight into museums and not serve progress and life? Or is it the day's excessive demand for artistic renewal in leaps that has forced him out into this convulsive attempt to behave differently? The de-

ERIK HANSEN

This spread: This chair was designed by Finn Juhl for Bovirke in 1953. It was the first chair he designed that was decidedly suited to industrial manufacture. The shelf piece atop the back legs is at normal table height. It can be used as an armrest in different sitting positions. The chair was produced in the United States by Baker Furniture, Inc.

51

YOSHIO HAYASHI

mand for new things to proclaim in the press, the demand for new things to make a show at new exhibitions, can turn even those who sit highest, because of their undeniable artistic talent, into weathervanes."

Børge Mogensen sent Finn Juhl the article before it was published, and the periodical's editors asked him for a comment. So he sat down and wrote the following:

Dear Pen Pals: A. Karlsen, B. Mogensen,   *December 6, 1961*
Has a religious war broken out?
The angry, obstinate Arne Karlsen has hitched Børge Mogensen to his wagon and is racing like Thor over the heavens, dealing out blows in the face with his hammer to all dissenters. Thunder, and lightning that smells like sulphur.
There is no doubt that you will end up as a constellation!
As [the Norwegian author Bjørnstjerne] Bjørnson wrote, "Let us have a friendly chat." What do you use the Cabinetmakers' Guild exhibition for?
Børge Mogensen lived up to last year since he showed the same furniture on a folded up tapestry by Vibeke Klint in the exhibition's darkest room.
Previously he showed a very deep sofa with bolsters which position the victim properly. Today it is being produced and can certainly bring the hem of any virtuous lady up to hip or shoulder height if she should wish to leave the piece. It is advertised amusingly as suitable for a soccer team, and who would not love to have one in his home? No one is out after publicity here. This is a sound, sensible basic philosophy.
This year Arne Karlsen showed a cabinet (where was the key?) whose hinges were constructed in such a way that the doors could only be opened and closed with the tolerance of ± 1 cm. used in masonry. Your sanctimonious indignation [should be seen] against this background. Don't set your clay feet out in the rain!

YOSHIO HAYASHI

This spread: Armchair designed for Bovirke in 1953. It is a variation, suited to industrial manufacture, of a chair designed in 1946 for Niels Vodder and shown at the Cabinetmakers' Guild exhibition the same year.

Remember [the Danish poet Johan Herman] Wessel's song: "To benefit, be kind: always bear in mind," and don't forget the first verb. There is nothing in the song about blowing your own horn.
Yours very sincerely,
Finn Juhl

He did not, however, send the letter, so it is published here for the first time.

But there were others who countered the unbalanced criticism of Karlsen and Mogensen, including the author of this book. The director of the Danish Society of Arts and Crafts, the witty Bent Salicath with the mordant pen, wrote in the Society's periodical, "With the last cleaning of the temple at the Cabinetmakers' Guild exhibition – and for that matter within arts and crafts and decorative art as a whole – which Børge Mogensen and Arne Karlsen undertook jointly last year in their fierce but stimulating sermon in Arkitekten (no. 1/62), Finn Juhl and several other well-known Danish designers were accused of indulging in vanities and foolery and voluptuous gluttony with expensive and rare types of wood. Modernism's sinners were given chapter and verse, and many had their eyes opened by this sermon to how far we had sunk into sin here at home [in Denmark] in the field of design. It did not help anything that the 6th commandment had been broken with perfect grace."[12]

ERIK HANSEN

Easy chair designed for Bovirke, probably in 1954. It was a variation of the "45 Chair" suited to industrial manufacture. The crossed rungs are an elegant touch that give the chair great stability.

LOUIS SCHNAKENBURG

The furniture at the Cabinetmakers' Guild exhibition in 1961 which sparked off the attack on Finn Juhl by Arne Karlsen and Børge Mogensen. The furniture was intended for a bedroom. The low chairs with gun-metal colored legs and frame of cherry had sturdy cushions and back bolsters covered with Thai silk. The little chest of drawers was also made of cherry, with drawers painted in different colors. The low table had the same frame as the chairs, but no cushions or bolsters. The large bed, also of cherry, had painted panels. The whole interior was made by cabinetmaker Ludvig Pontoppidan, since Finn Juhl's long-term collaboration with Niels Vodder had ceased at this point. The sculpture is by Erik Thommesen and the painting by Vilhelm Lundstrøm – two artists whom Finn Juhl greatly admired.

Later in the article he wrote, "Polemicists can join the slaughter-house atmosphere that prevails when named coryphaei are being butchered, and feel satisfaction when the cuts are deep and sure, but for my part, I feel that far too many of the cuts and carvings which Karlsen-Mogensen made were too unsure: too much slashing at random. It might be sensible to show the dangers of a trend and to turn against the followers of a certain form of expression or a certain goal. But there is something wrong in the critics' aim when they want to bring down Finn Juhl, Jens Quistgaard, Ib Kofod-Larsen, Verner Panton, etc. with one shot and view the work of these highly diverse persons as being typical of today's situation in design."

Through a discussion of that year's Cabinetmakers' Guild exhibition, Bent Salicath then took a stand on a number of the claims that Karlsen and Mogensen made in their article.

Finn Juhl took the attack from the humorous side, as his letter shows, and although he was urged to, he did not start a serious debate with the two critics. But he never forgot that he had been called a weathervane that turns as the wind blows, something he returned to several times in interviews later on. If it bothered him a bit, it was probably because his furniture at the exhibition in 1961 *was* indeed an attempt to travel new roads. At this time he was aware that he was unable to continue in the idiom he had used so far – among other things because his furniture had been so thoroughly copied and plagiarized. He viewed the attack by Karlsen and Mogensen as unjust because, as he said, "If the Cabinetmakers' Guild competitions and exhibitions are not to be used for experimentation, what use are they?" His chairs at the exhibition in 1961 *were* an experiment (they incidentally won a prize), and the fact that an artist seeks new forms of expression for his talent is not in any way odious. They did not, however, lead to the regeneration of his idiom.

It also vexed him that it was so often claimed that he exaggerated the artistic expression of his furniture. As an architect, he was a child of functionalism, so for him utility was the primary requirement. It did not, however, necessarily have to lead to an indifferent form. He considered it precisely the task of designers to make form into an expressive part of function. He also considered it completely natural for the applied artist to seek inspiration from the fine art of his day – and not from the idioms of the past. He himself admitted that he had been inspired by modern sculpture's analytical work with bodies in free and bound movement, as he found in contemporary work by Hans Arp, Barbara Hepworth, Henry Moore, Giacometti, etc., and also in the moving sculptures, mobiles, of Alexander Calder.

"The craftsman's ability to form is probably the same as that of a sculptor. A chair is not just a product of decorative art in a space; it is a form and a space in itself," he wrote in 1952.[13]

It was this attitude that led to the misconception that he considered his furniture to be sculptures of a kind, probably also because the different parts of his furniture often had sculptural contours. "I ask not to be misunderstood: furniture is furniture, not sculpture. But both fields involve the work of giving form," he said in a lecture at the Danish Society of Crafts and Design in 1949, a lecture that was later printed in the Society's periodical.[14]

This page: Easy chair and sofa designed for Bovirke. The chair was the first piece of furniture that Finn Juhl designed for the company. It was launched in 1952, made of beech with palisander insets in the armrests.

Opposite page: Panel wall and table bench designed for Bovirke. The panel wall was available with painted panels or panels veneered with various types of wood. The table bench had a frame of oxidized metal and brass molding along the side to prevent the cushions from sliding off when the bench was used as a seat.

ERIK HANSEN

KELD HELMER-PETERSEN

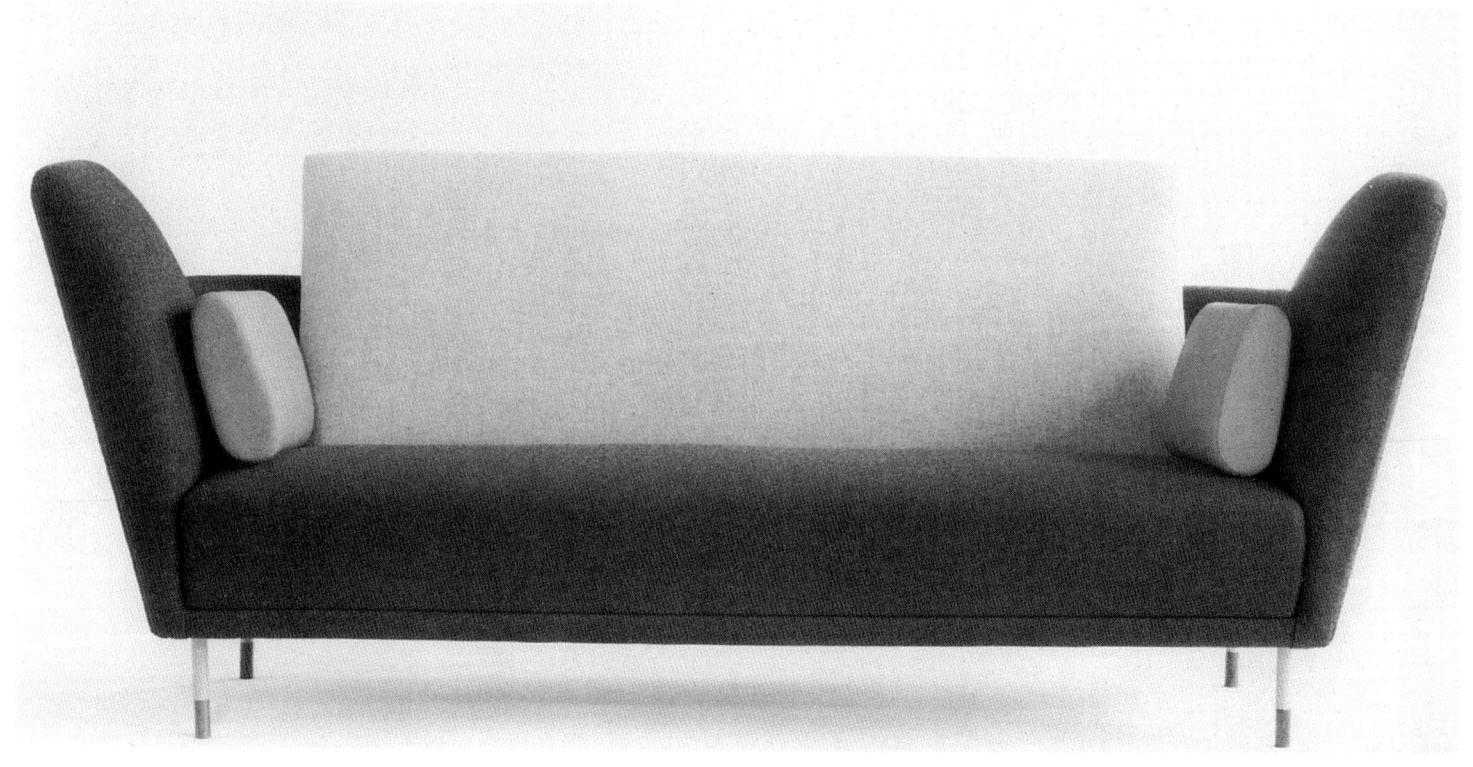

ERIK HANSEN

ERIK HANSEN

57

YOSHIO HAYASHI

YOSHIO HAYASHI

This spread: Easy chair made by Niels Vodder for the Cabinetmakers' Guild exhibition in 1953. As the drawing shows, Finn Juhl intended for the chair to be covered with cowhide, but it was always produced with a cloth upholstery.

HVILESTOL
SNEDKERLAUGETS UDSTILLING 1953
FINN JUHL, ARKITEKT M.A.A.
NYHAVN 33, KØBENHAVN K.
DATO: 20 AUGUST 1953
MÅL: 1:4
RETTET

59

ERIK HANSEN

This spread: Director's office designed by Finn Juhl for C.W.F. France at France & Daverkosen's factory in Ørholm. The factory was actually a mattress factory, but Mr. France got the idea that it could also make cushions for chairs and sofas. He asked Finn Juhl, among others, to design some furniture suited to the purpose. Both chairs shown were first produced in 1953. The chair on the right was the first industrially manufactured chair made of teak.

ERIK HANSEN

LOUIS SCHNAKENBURG

Opposite page: A shelf system, desk, and armchair in the "Diplomat Range" which Finn Juhl developed for France & Søn in 1961-62.

This page: Large easy chair, designed for France & Søn at the same time as the "Diplomat Range." It was marketed under the exotic name of "Bwana," and was undoubtedly intended as an industrially manufactured parallel to the "Chieftain Chair." It completely lacked its elegance, however, and was not a commercial success.

ERIK HANSEN

After Poul Cadovius's company Royal System had taken over France & Søn's models, including those designed by Finn Juhl, he made several designs for the company at the end of the 1960s and beginning of the '70s, only a few of which were produced. The drawings show designs made in 1967 for link chairs of oxidized metal and plywood intended for public areas and designs for a shelf and cabinet system made in 1974. This was the last furniture design made by Finn Juhl.

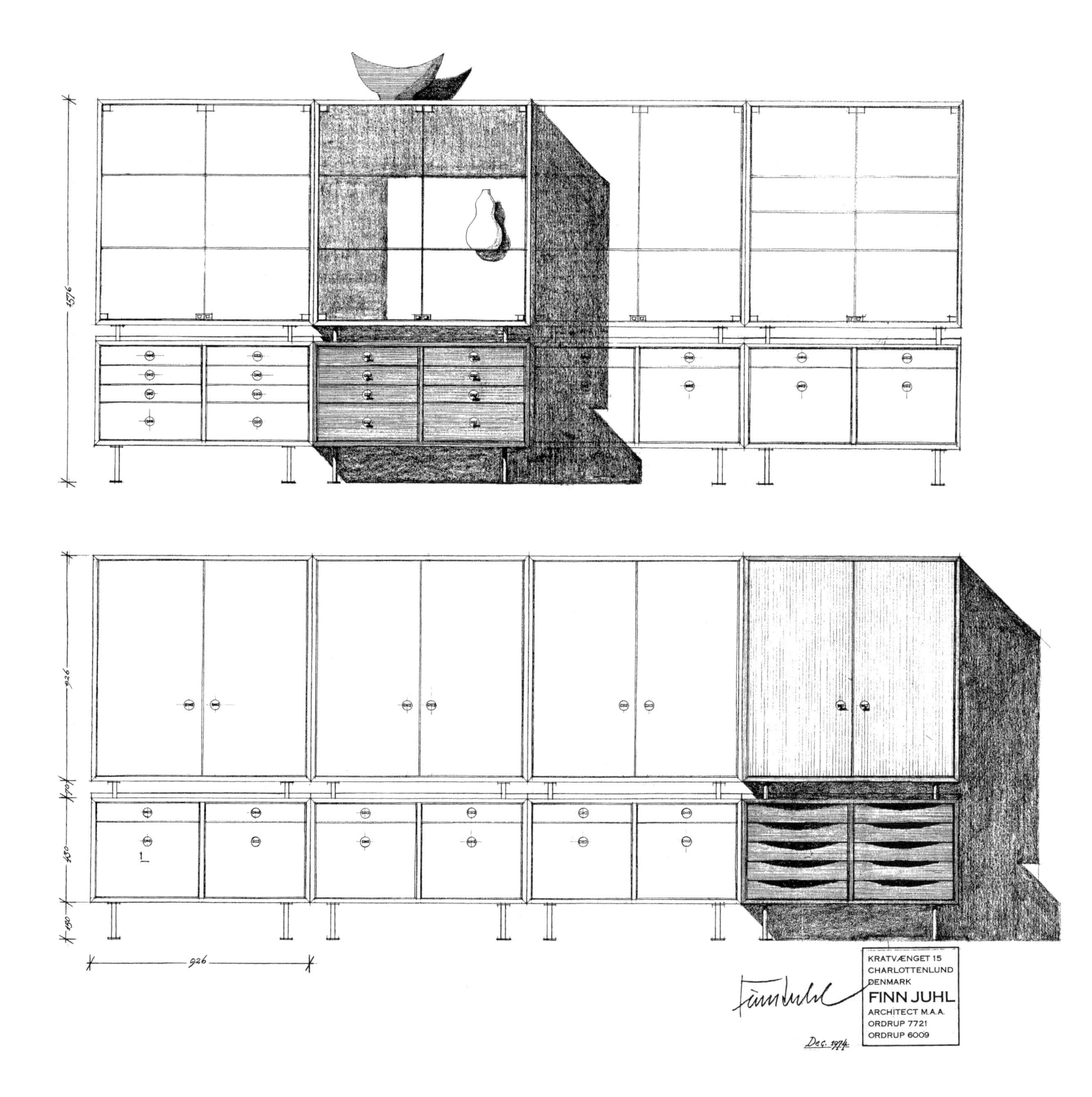

KRATVÆNGET 15
CHARLOTTENLUND
DENMARK
FINN JUHL
ARCHITECT M.A.A.
ORDRUP 7721
ORDRUP 6009

Dec. 1974

GUTENBERGHUS

INTERIORS

The Bing & Grøndahl store

Finn Juhl's first major interior design project was the Bing & Grøndahl Porcelain Manufactory store on Copenhagen's Amagertorv Square. The special thing about this store was that no counters were used. The products were to be placed on shelves, on tables, or in showcases, as in an exhibition. The only piece of ordinary store equipment was a packing counter with a cash register, one on each of the two floors.

The upper floor was to hold the table services and a room for changing exhibitions, while the ground floor, as before, was to have a section for art porcelain and stoneware. In the plans it was of decisive importance that the public be made aware that something could also be found on the upper floor, at the same time avoiding making the rooms on the ground floor into only antechambers.

The store consisted all in all of five rooms linked by portals and a stairwell. The rooms lay at angles and had different heights and degrees of lighting. This is why Finn Juhl did not try to create a unifying feeling of space, but instead dealt with each room in turn, with transitions from one room to the next clearly marked with panels. An effort was made to create a feeling of unity through the treatment of materials and use of colors.

In a store with so many products of more or less the same size and character as porcelain and stoneware, it is important that furnishings make it possible to create visual variation. All backboards in the showcases and all wall panels could thus be either turned or replaced, giving them a variety of colors or veneers. The exhibition tables were of highly different shapes, heights, and constructions, also making it possible to vary the exhibition.

The choice of materials and colors was carefully considered. Porcelain in itself has such a cool, aloof character that it is necessary to create a background that can give it a greater feeling of warmth than porcelain provides. This is why Finn Juhl chose teak for tables and shelves – not varnished, it should be noted, but oiled and mat – and for wall panels woven bast, perhaps also because these materials provided an association with "China."

The colors of the rooms, which had to suit both porcelain and stoneware at the same time, had to be kept in delicate tones. An exception was the green ceiling in the first entrance room on the ground floor, where the enormous height of the room made it necessary to choose a radical treatment, and the Venice red opening wall on the upper floor. As a contrast to the sobriety in the choice of materials and colors, some of the tables had varnished tray tops in bluish-green, Chinese lacquer red, and green.

Opposite page: The Bing & Grøndahl store facade on Amagertorv Square was designed by Finn Juhl when the store was expanded in 1963. It was not an easy task, since the windows had different breadths and depths, and the entrance to the other storeys in the building cuts into the facade between two windows. But the broad gray stone band and the narrow aluminum band above the door made it possible to keep the highly heterogeneous parts together. The completely uniform covering of the plinth and the columns with almost black marble also helped give a unified impression to the facade.

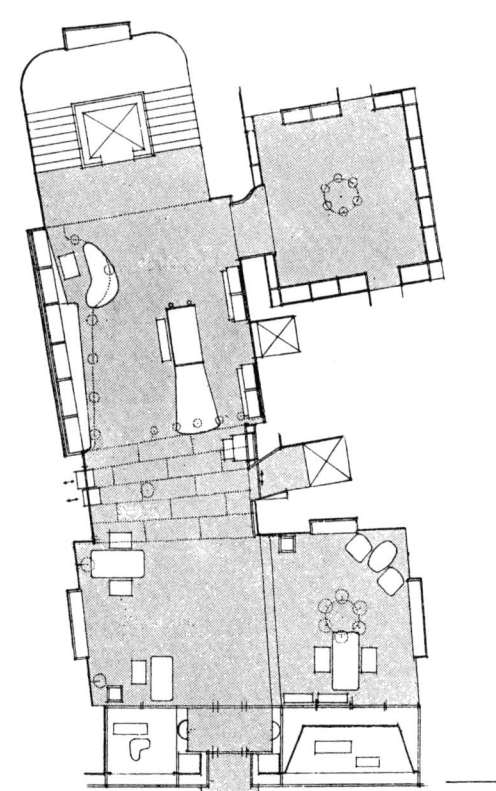

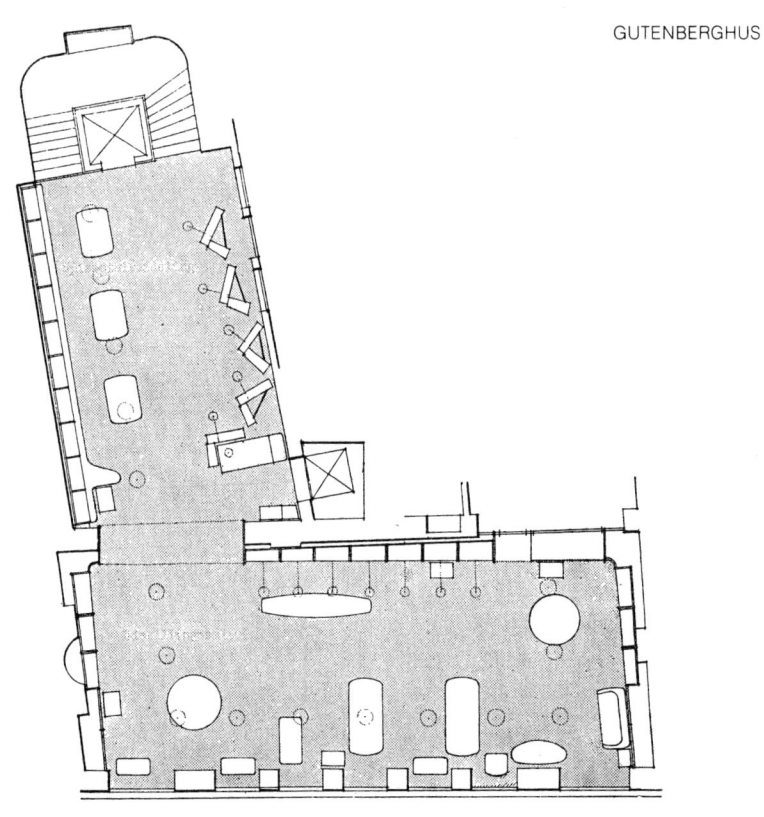

GUTENBERGHUS

GUTENBERGHUS

GUTENBERGHUS

All of the lighting fixtures were specially designed for the project by Finn Juhl, with the exception of the opal glass globes which had been designed by Vilhelm Lauritzen for the Radio Building.

Opposite page: The interior of the store on the ground floor seen towards the staircase and elevator. The portal between the two rooms in the store was covered with panels of Oregon pine. The drawings are on a scale of 1: 200.
This page: Exhibition rooms on the first floor.

The Trusteeship Council Chamber in New York

The Trusteeship Council, whose meeting room Finn Juhl was commissioned to furnish in 1950, was one of the United Nations' permanent councils, whose task it was to administer previous colonies on their way to independence which were temporarily under the trusteeship of the United Nations under a governor general.

In carrying out this project, Finn Juhl had to take account of the fact that the architecture of United Nations headquarters was highly modern and fairly unconventional and that diplomacy and the art of statesmanship at the U.N. are acted out unconventionally and open to public scrutiny. The council chambers can thus to a certain extent be compared to work premises, but also to theaters, where the press, radio, and television ensure that everyone takes part in the performance.

The chamber that Finn Juhl was commissioned to furnish was the middle of three identical chambers. It was not particularly well proportioned: about 42 meters long, 23 meters wide, and 8 meters high. Finn Juhl immediately felt it was too low in relation to the other proportions. It had a glass wall at the end with an impressive view of the East River. But this meant that the chamber had a strong backlight on everyone placed facing the window. The floor space was apportioned so that the area against the east wall was set aside for the delegates and their staff, while the amphitheater-like construction behind it was intended for the press and the public. The two side walls had entrances and two long rows of windows, one over the other, behind which there were rooms for interpreters, TV, etc. "There is no feeling or definition of space," Finn Juhl noted after he had seen the chamber.

After he returned home from New York, he evidently vacationed in Italy, since the first sketches of how this very difficult room was to take shape are dated Positano, July 12, 1950. Even though these are the first rough drawings, they show that Finn Juhl was already aware of how the project should be carried out. The final form of the room is very close to that given in these sketches (page 74). This is a typical work method for an architect: after having seen the area where the project is to be carried out, he imagines how it should be done, after which he tries to set down his idea on a note pad, and if he is certain that it is the right one, he sticks to it as far as possible in later drawings.

Finn Juhl also sketched out the delegates' chairs in Positano on July 27, 1950, and the sketch only differs a little from the final chair (pages 74 and 75).

The final arrangement, as shown in the sketches, was that the places for the delegates and the press were marked with the help of gently curved paneled side walls and a very unusual ceiling construction, while the walls and ceiling of the public area were only plastered and painted. The curved side walls were covered with molded slats of Oregon pine which to a certain extent regulate the acoustics.

The special formation of the ceiling was chosen because Finn Juhl considered the ceiling too low. This is why he rejected the usual choice of a dropped ceiling, which would hide the installations for the electrical and ventilation fittings, etc. This was what was done in the other two chambers, and the low ceilings over the delegates'

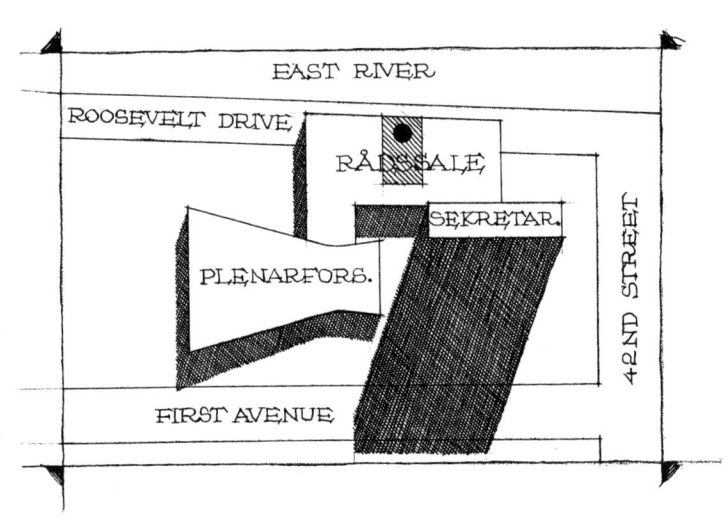

Opposite page: Trusteeship Council Chamber seen from the visitors' area. The delegates sat at the horseshoe-shaped table with their backs to the light. Behind the delegates' chairs, which were designed by Finn Juhl, were two rows of built-in chairs for the delegates' staffs. These chairs were standard models designed by the U.N.'s architect's office. The long table had room for the secretariat's staff and special experts. Their chairs were designed by Finn Juhl.

This page: Sketch showing the location of the Trusteeship Council Chamber.

J. W. MOLITOR

This spread: Longitudinal section and cross section of the Council Chamber on a scale of c. 1: 100 and floor plan on a scale of c. 1: 250.

72

73

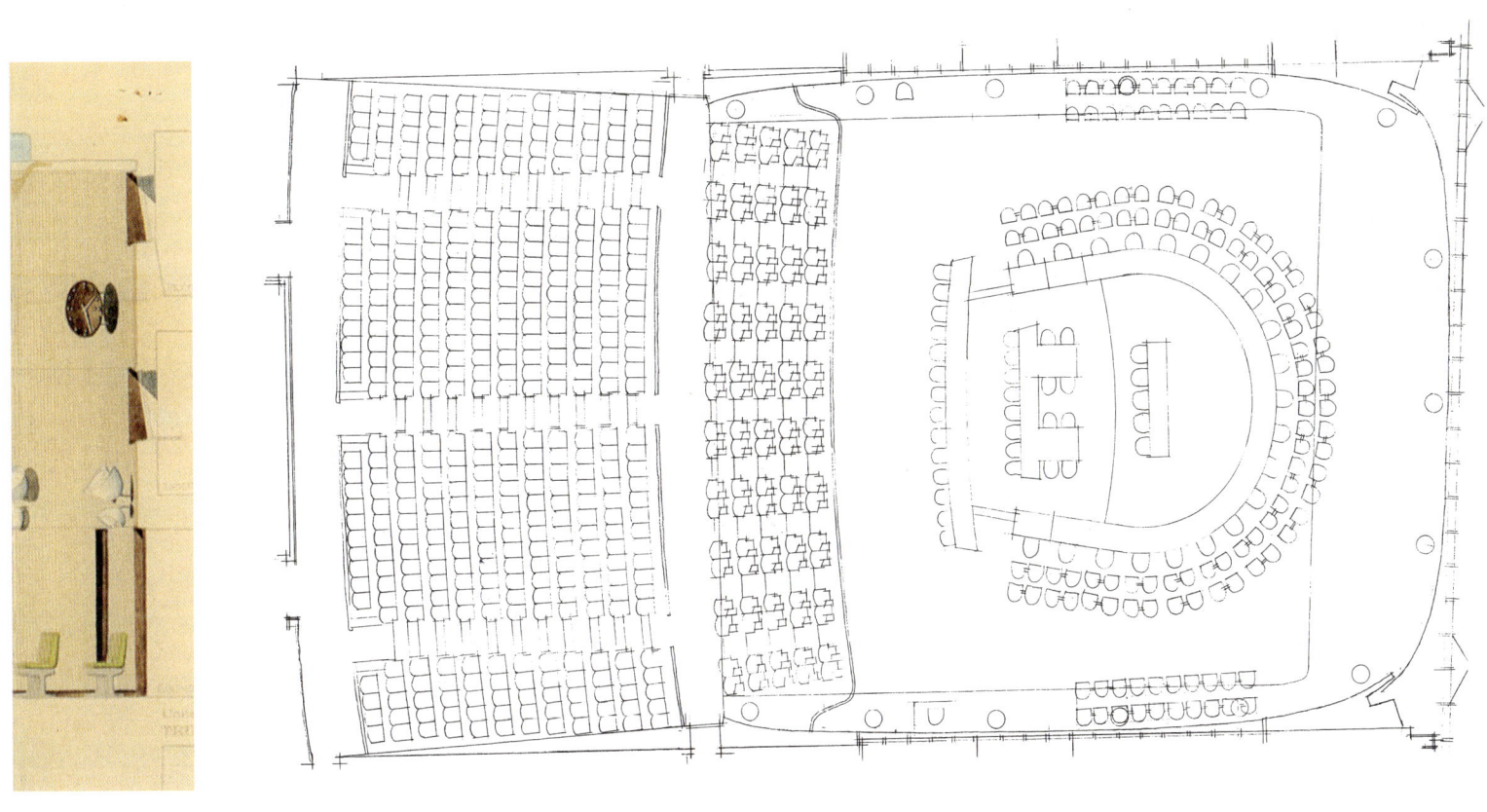

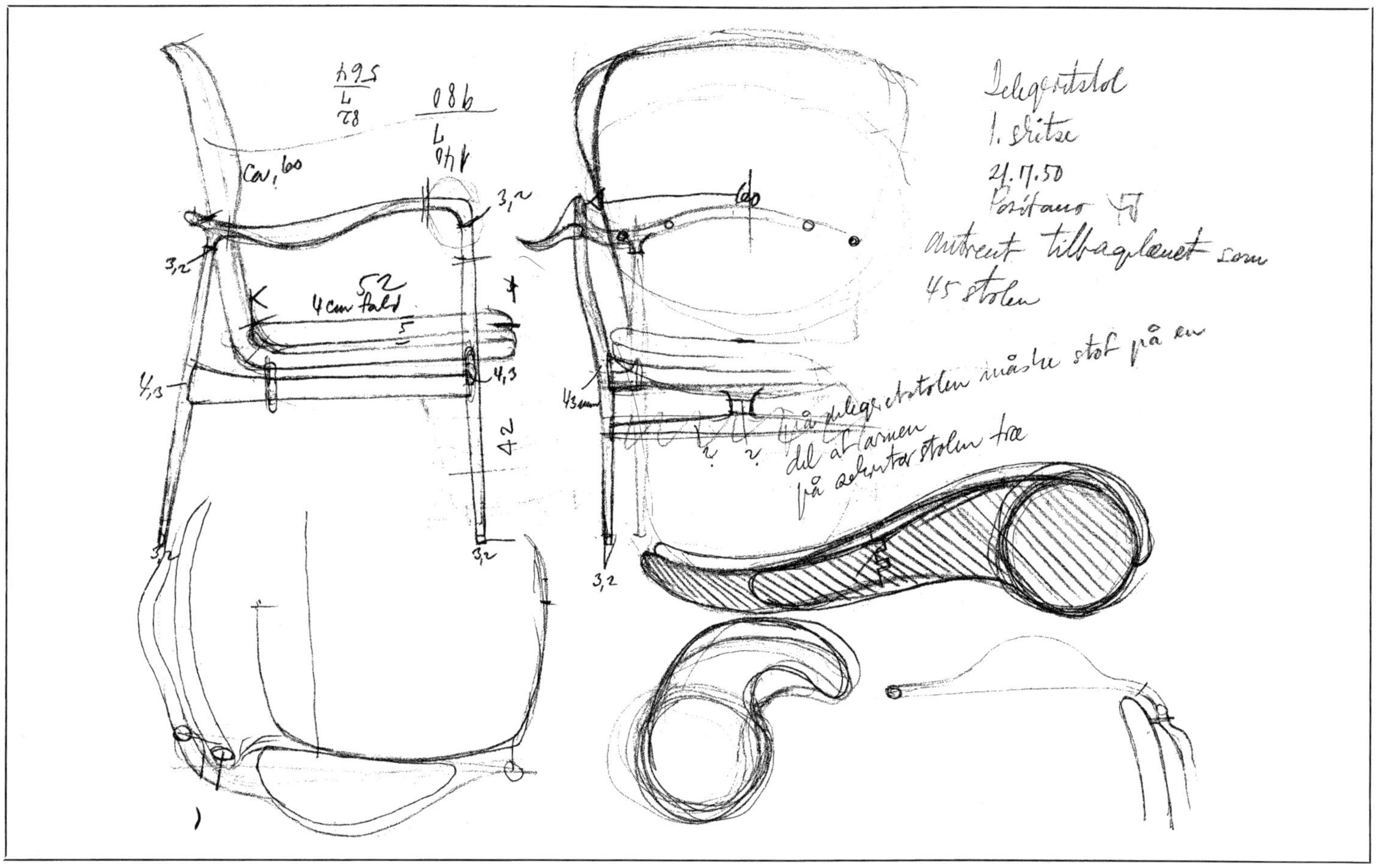

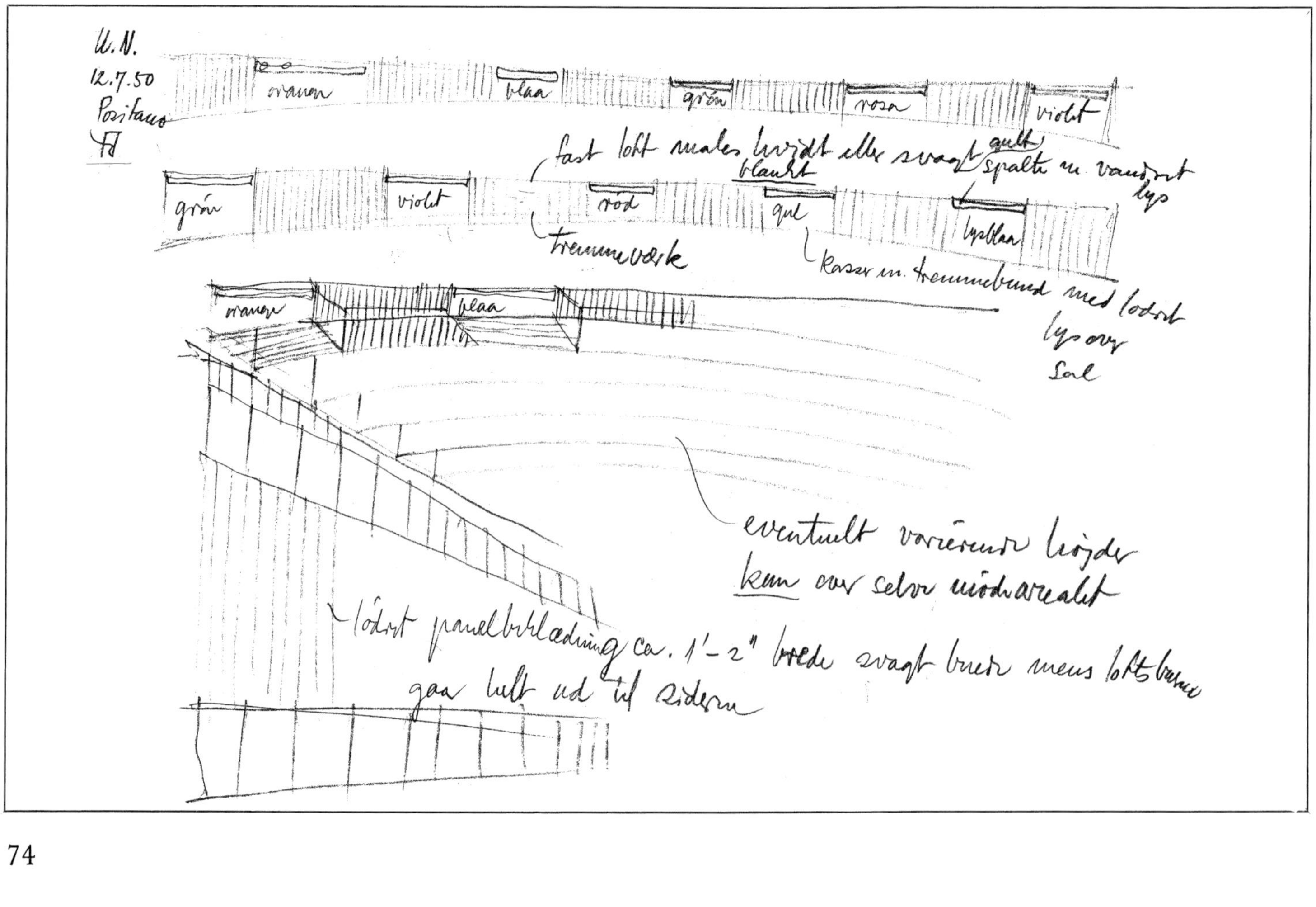

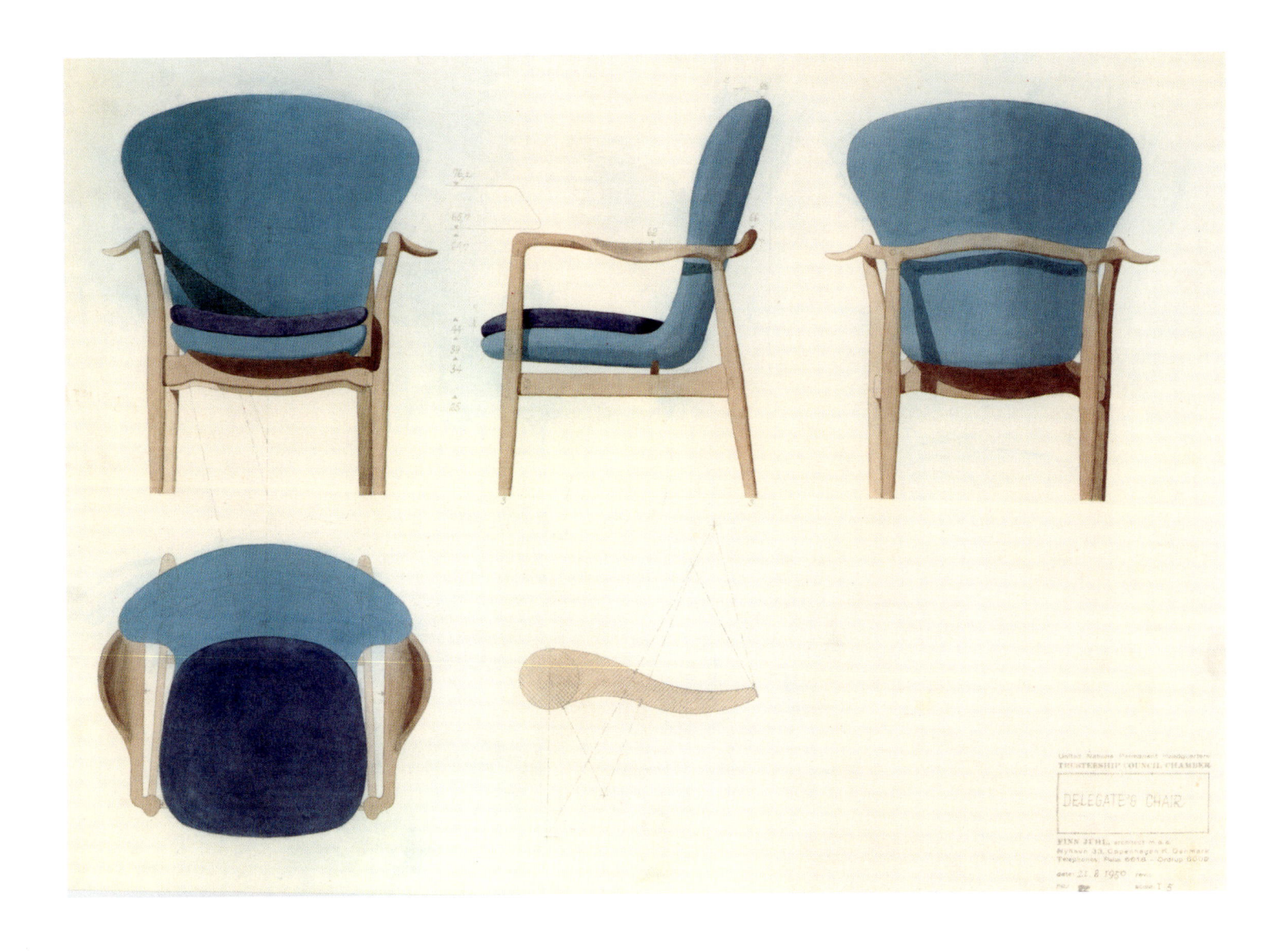

Opposite page: Finn Juhl's first sketches of the Council Chamber and the delegates' chairs, made in Positano, Italy, on July 12 and 21, 1950, respectively.

This page: Drawing for delegates' chair. Niels Vodder made a prototype in this design, which was shown at the Cabinetmakers' Guild exhibition in 1950, but Finn Juhl was not satisfied with it. He consequently reworked it, giving it a lower back and another form for the back leg. It was shown at the Cabinetmakers' Guild exhibition the following year and was a far lovelier chair. See the photograph on page 10 and the design on page 47.

seats indeed seem oppressive. (The author had the opportunity to see the three chambers in 1960.)

Finn Juhl's choice was a ceiling construction consisting of 30 hanging, perforated screens held by boxes for lighting and ventilation equipment. The ceiling's upper level, which was covered with acoustic board, was painted a shiny light blue, while the lower level was marked by shiny metal runners with two slight curves fastened to the boxes. The long sides of these boxes were of perforated iron sheeting painted six different colors in an irregular pattern. "The colors do not attempt to create any symbolism of national flags," Finn Juhl wrote. "On the other hand, they do give the impression of flags that are hung for a ceremony or other festive occasion, such as the flags in the cathedral of Sienna."

Finn Juhl's intention in his design for the ceiling was to dissolve the precise impression of the ceiling plane by constructing a spheric, hovering, three-dimensional ceiling in order to create an airy and festive chamber. And he truly succeeded.

Finn Juhl designed two types of chair for the chamber, one with armrests for delegates, and one without for their staff of officials and secretaries. Sixty-two of them were made by cabinetmaker Niels Vodder. The built-in chairs for the press and public were a standard model designed by the United Nations architects' office. Finn Juhl also designed the parapet for the delegates' area, doors, fitted tables, a rug, a clock, and lighting fixtures. The large woolen curtain for the glass wall was woven by the Danish weaver Paula Trock at Spindegården in Askov.

The sculpture on the northern side wall was made by Henrik Starcke (1898–1973). It was carved out of teak and painted, and symbolizes man's wish for freedom.

The chamber was inaugurated at a meeting on February 27, 1952, at which the Trusteeship Council was gathered and declared it its permanent home.

UNITED NATIONS

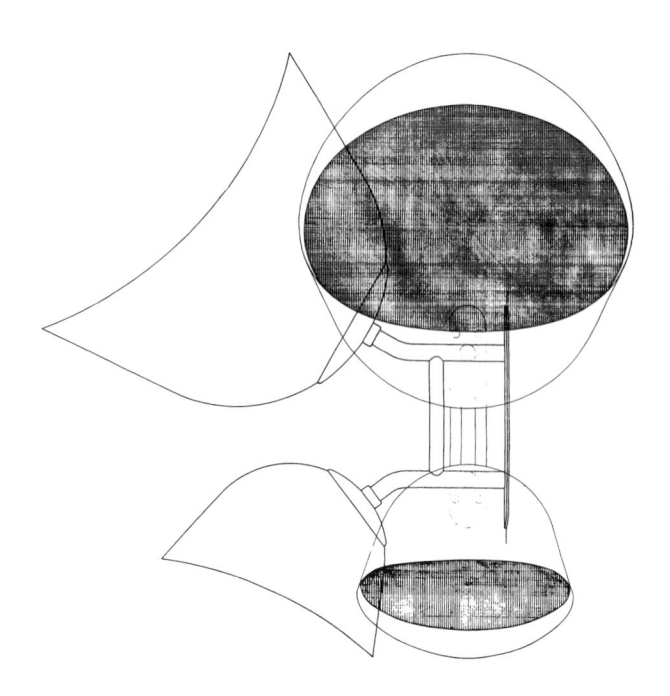

76

Opposite page: Above, Henrik Starcke's wooden sculpture, symbolizing mankind's wish for freedom. Below, the double lamp of brushed brass designed by Finn Juhl. Drawing on a scale of 1: 10.
This page: The chair for the secretariat's staff and special experts. The drawing shows the chair of maple and teak as it was made by Baker Furniture, Inc., to be sold in the United States. The chair was made for the U.N. by Niels Vodder completely in walnut and with upholstery in other colors.

"Interior 52" in Trondheim

In 1952, the Norwegian art historian T. Krohn-Hansen, who was head of the Nordenfjeldske Museum of Applied Art in Trondheim, asked Finn Juhl to furnish an exhibition room at the museum with modern decorative art. The idea was to create a room which was typical of the interior style of the middle of our own century as a supplement to the museum's William Morris room, which showed the style in the middle of the 19th century, and the Henry van de Velde room, which marked the turn of the century. The museum now wanted a Finn Juhl room.

The room that was put at Finn Juhl's disposal was not exciting. It was, in fact, exceedingly dismal, long and narrow, 3.30 × 6.80 meters, and with two ordinary windows on the long side. Finn Juhl did, however, manage to get the museum to grant money to expand it with a bay window 4 meters wide and 1.10 meter deep, creating a glass wall the whole height of the room and the full breadth of the bay window, opening up an excellent view of the city's rooftops and the fjord. He also had a narrow light opening made, again the height of the room, just to the right of the entrance.

At the end of the room, a panel wall of Oregon pine was set up, while the ceiling and floor were covered with exquisite Kalmar pine. The entrance wall was painted a deep green to create just as precise a definition of the room on this end as the panel wall did on the other. A wooden sculpture, "Two People," by Erik Thommesen, was placed at the transition point between the narrow and the broad parts of the room.

In addition to Finn Juhl's own furniture, the room was furnished with a chair by Charles Eames, two of Alvar Aalto's stools, and a little palisander table by the Dane Peder Moos. The rug was made by the Swedish weaver Barbro Nilsson, and the curtains, of light spun wool, were made by Paula Trock. A couple of the showcases on the paneled wall were used to exhibit a complete set of the Dane Kay Bojesen's "Grand Prix" silverware and a porcelain table service by the Norwegian designer Tias Eckhoff. The shelves held stoneware by the Dane Axel Salto and others.

KELD HELMER-PETERSEN

Opposite page: "Interior 52" at the Nordenfjeldske Museum of Applied Art seen looking toward the panel wall, and floor plan on a scale of 1: 50.
This page: The room seen looking towards the entrance. The furniture in the sofa group was held together by its use of color. The sofa seat has turquoise and ultramarine stripes and the chair seat is of the same turquoise blue. The sofa and chair backs are in a neutral gray with a bold structure to the fabric.

SVEIN LIAN

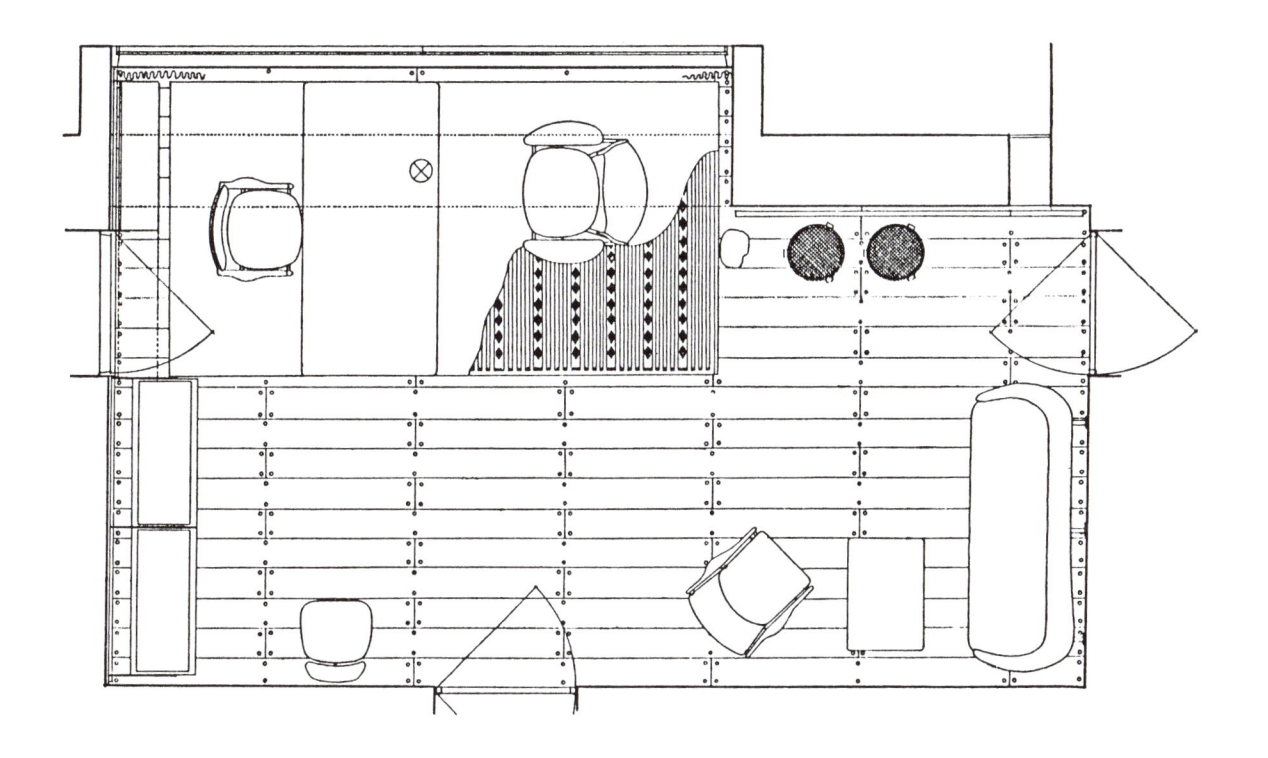

Villabyernes Bio

The Villabyernes Bio movie theater in Vangede, north of Copenhagen, which Finn Juhl designed in 1955 for Mogens Fisker, no longed exists, like so much of his work. It was a large cubic building of shiny yellow brick without windows, from which the low foyer jutted out like a separate structure. Five steps led to the theater's entrance, which lay on the center line of the building. When one came from the fairly small, low-ceilinged foyer and looked right down through the theater, it seemed very large and light, a well-calculated effect. As soon as one entered the theater, the eye was caught by a large yellow curtain, which covered the whole breadth of the end wall. From the entrance, the floor fell in a curve down towards the middle of the room and then rose again towards the proscenium. This curved line was clearly delineated by a hand rail along the side wall – like a railing on a ship.

The panels on the long walls had several functions. They were set up partly to provide the right acoustics, partly as a decoration, and

This spread: Villabyernes Bio movie theater. Longitudinal section, on a scale of 1:100.
This page: Facade towards Vangedevej.
Opposite page: Theater and floor plan on a scale of 1:250.

KELD HELMER-PETERSEN

KELD HELMER-PETERSEN

they were also the background for the room's general lighting, since a little cylindrical lamp was placed in one corner of each. The panels came in three sizes and were either painted white, light blue, ultramarine, or orange, or decorated with photographs by Keld Helmer-Petersen. These black and white nature photographs almost seemed abstract, producing a clear decorative effect.

Villabyernes Bio was a good example that Finn Juhl was able to create a room that seemed large with the use of limited, inexpensive materials. Except for the panels and pine boards on the back part of the long walls (which also had an acoustic function), the walls were plastered and painted with oil-based paint. The floor was made of simple pine planks with cocoanut matting on the outer aisles and carpeting on the center aisle. The whole spacial effect was determined by the room's clearly defined form and the light, finely harmonized colors. It is regrettable that the theater no longer exists. In the 1970s, when competition from television killed the big movie theaters, Villabyernes Bio also suffered its demise.

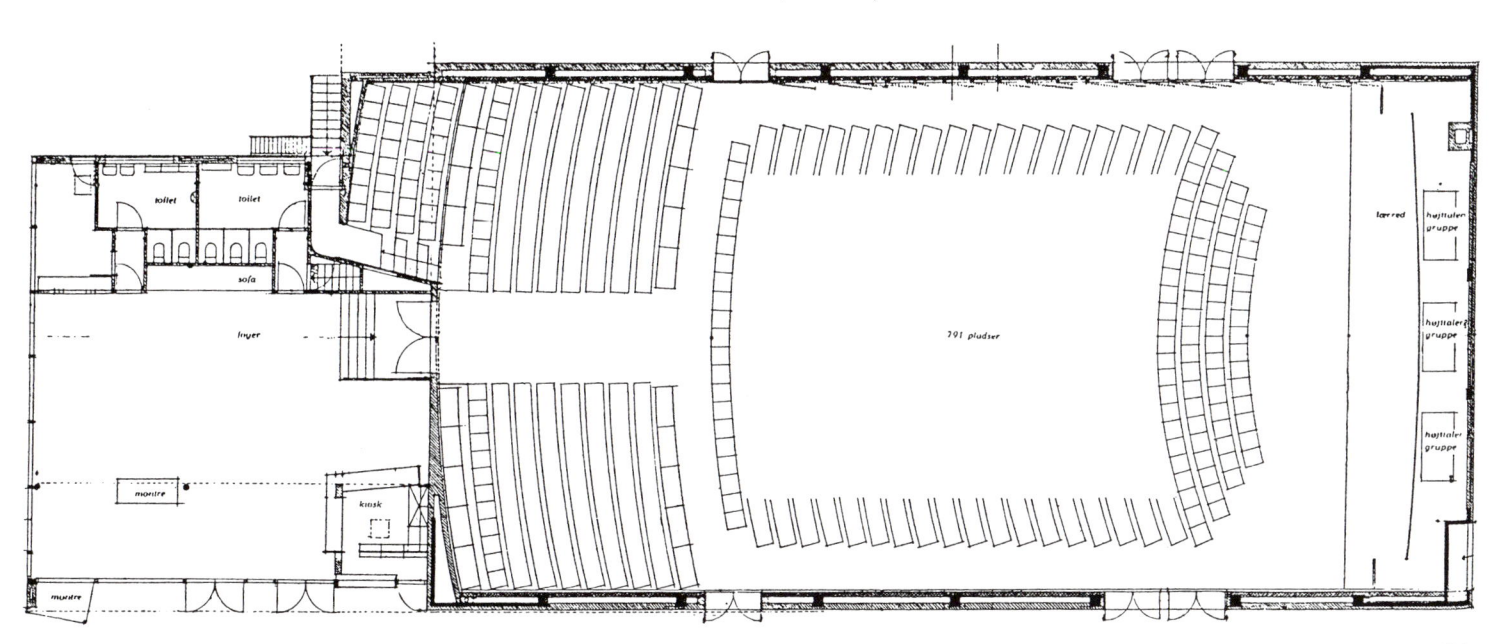

Ticket offices for SAS

It was an enormous commission Finn Juhl was given in 1956 when SAS asked him to take charge of furnishing the company's ticket offices. It was a major project and also a difficult one. The offices were spread throughout Europe and Asia, in rented premises of highly diverse character. Some of them already existed, while others had to be opened first. The former had been furnished very much at random, with highly different furnishings. They had to be remodeled one after the other. The offices that had to be created from scratch were naturally the most interesting projects. The architect was able to make more of his own mark on the interior.

In addition to creating offices that were able to function in practice, it was Finn Juhl's task to give all SAS offices a uniform look that as far as possible would distinguish them from the ticket offices of other airlines. SAS wanted to have an image which immediately gave the impression of quality. Here it was natural for Finn Juhl to build upon the Nordic tradition of arts and crafts which at that very time had won an international reputation under the designation of "Scandinavian design." The use of carefully finished fine woods, light, airy textiles, attention to details, and simplicity of design were his means. Finn Juhl naturally first and foremost used his own furniture.

It was a logical beginning to work out standard designs for furnishings that could be used for all the necessary practical functions of issuing tickets, checking baggage, etc. The designs were so flexible that they could be suited to different offices with as few changes as possible contingent on local conditions.

It naturally took time to work out standard furnishings like these and for the first year or so Finn Juhl had to use *ad hoc* arrangements in the offices which had to be remodeled quickly. The first ticket office that was equipped with the new furnishings was in Gothenburg and opened in February 1958. Finn Juhl recommended that when sufficient experience had been gained from this office's function, a manual with designs and instructions for "an ideal SAS office" should be worked out to create the basis for furnishing future offices. A manual of this kind was something new at the time, though manuals are now found in many large enterprises. The recommendation was not followed.

KELD HELMER-PETERSEN

This spread: SAS ticket office in Gothenburg.

KELD HELMER-PETERSEN

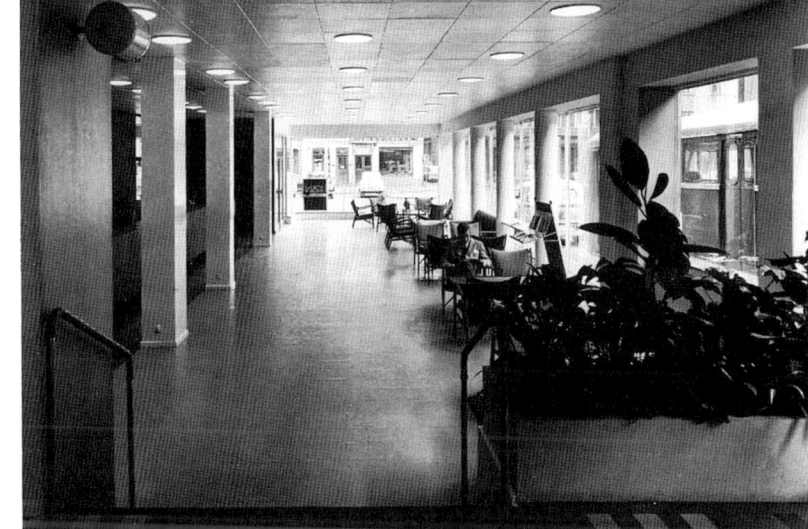

KELD HELMER-PETERSEN

It was naturally frustrating for a perfectionist like Finn Juhl that he could never be certain that the offices were furnished down to the last detail according to his ideas and in keeping with his designs. In his design office's monthly reports to SAS headquarters in Stockholm, he often complained about this state of affairs. On May 1, 1958, the following was written about the newly furnished office in Vienna: "It was very surprising to note the many divergences from the designs, descriptions, and agreements made. Becvar the architect has thus made altered designs for the counter with drawers, etc. that differ completely from the approved standard table that Finn Juhl designed."

For practical and economic reasons, furnishings often had to be made by local furniture factories, and it was difficult for Finn Juhl to ensure that they were correctly made and had a sufficiently high quality. He himself traveled to the most important cities several months each year to check the situation, and what he was unable to do was done by his closest collaborator, the architect Bo Cock-Clausen. But it was impossible to check everything, and he thus endeavored in many cases to work together with the local architects who supervised the work for him. This naturally required their loyalty, and most of them gave it. The architect in Vienna was one of the less fortunate cases.

As far as can be seen from the design office's monthly reports to SAS headquarters in Stockholm, Finn Juhl was responsible for furnishing the following ticket offices:

1957: Alexandria, Karachi, Baghdad, Athens, Jakarta, Milan, Beirut, Cairo, Glasgow, Tehran, London, Oslo, Stockholm.
1958: Barcelona, Geneva, Manchester, Calcutta, Gothenburg, Vienna, Malmö, Johannesburg, Kuwait, Munich.
1959: Tokyo, Amsterdam, Bangkok, Budapest, Prague, Lahore, Nairobi.
1960: Nice, Paris, West Berlin.

The last work for SAS was completed in 1961. The colossal investment in new planes for the jet age made SAS reluctant to invest in new offices or modernize existing ones. But Finn Juhl's task was largely completed. In spite of all the difficulties, he managed to put

83

his stamp of quality on all the most important ticket offices on two continents.

Developments in air travel were extraordinarily rapid during the following decades. The flood of passengers grew and it became necessary in time to rebuild, expand, or move the many tickets offices. Today there is probably not a single SAS ticket office with Finn Juhl's original interiors.

DC-8 airplanes

In 1956, Finn Juhl was commissioned to furnish the 7 new DC-8 jet planes that SAS had ordered from Douglas in Cleveland, Ohio, for delivery in 1958. They were ordered literally sight unseen, since when the order was made, there was not a single plane ready: the model was just being developed. But SAS had good experiences with the Douglas DC-7 propeller planes, and all the major airlines wanted to fly the new jets first.

In December 1956, Finn Juhl went to the United States together with the Swedish designer Rune Monö, consultant for SAS headquarters in Stockholm, and his colleague, the Norwegian architect Jacob Kielland-Brandt, to see how far along the new plane had come. There was only one full-sized model (a mock-up) of the cabin in addition to a few test models of chairs, all of which were studied down to the last detail. Finn Juhl was told that the absolute deadline for all major dispositions in the cabin interior was July 26, 1957. This also included the choice of types of chair and materials, while colors did not have to be chosen until November 1957.

Douglas had developed a new type of chair that was to be offered all the airlines that bought the DC-8. Any other type of chair would cost the airline considerably more than the standard model, something of which Finn Juhl was informed several times. "This information almost took the form of a threat," Juhl noted in his diary.

Nonetheless, Finn Juhl considered changing precisely the type of chair to be used. It seemed to him that the standard arrangement of two and two or three and three was a stiff and uncomfortable one.

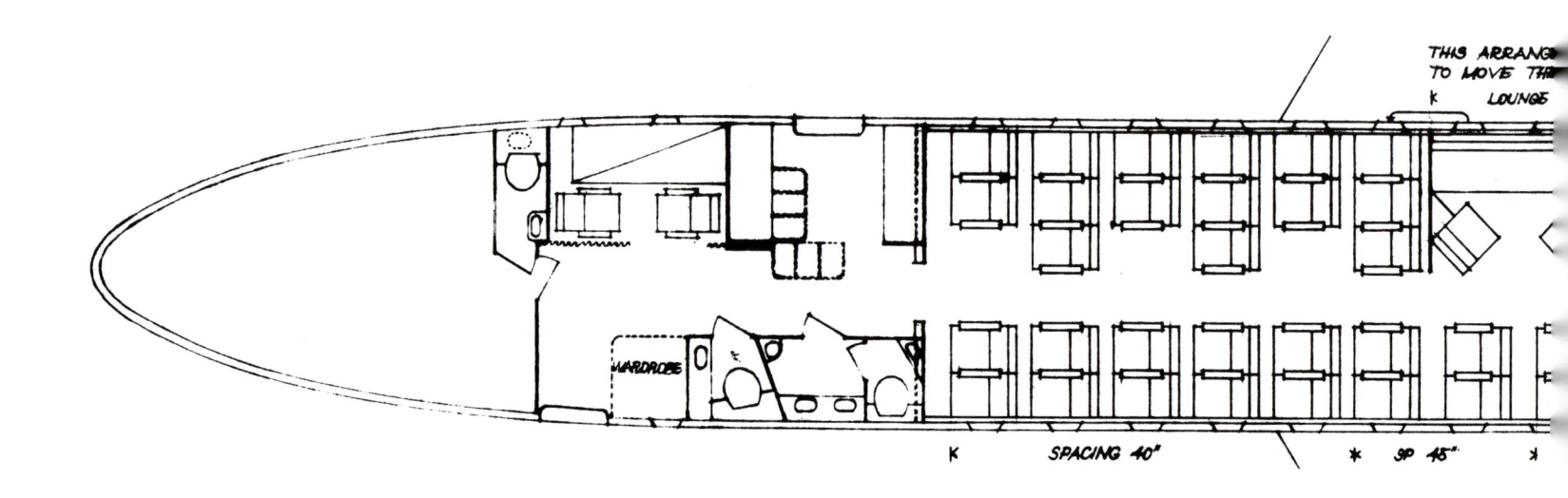

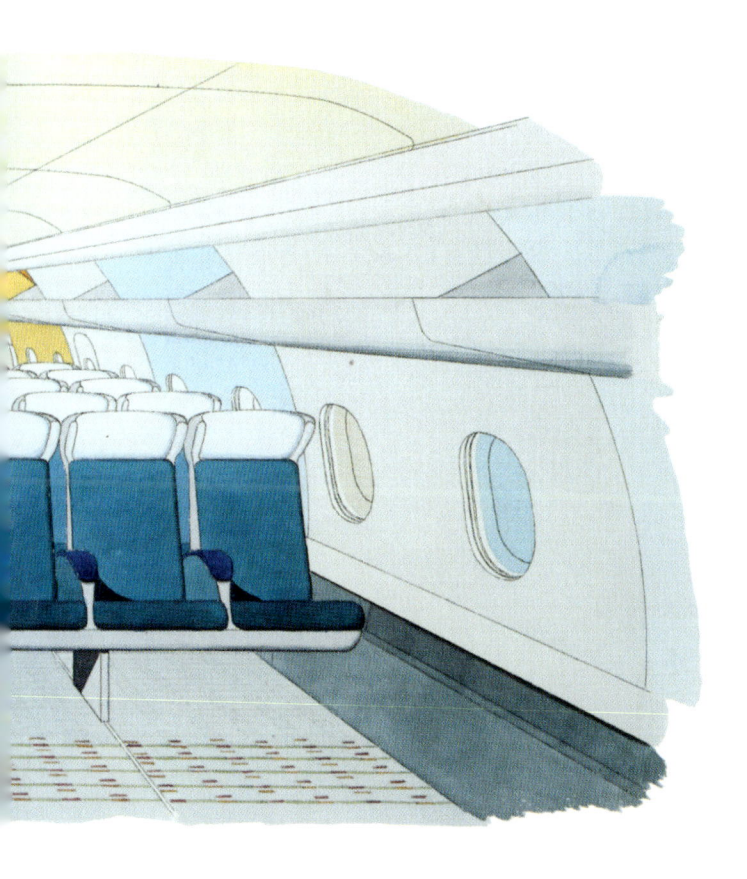

He consequently worked out a design by which swivel chairs in the first-class section were not placed in a straight line. This would make it easier for those not on the aisle to get in and out, and he felt that people would feel less locked in than if the chair were placed in a fixed position.

It is commendable that SAS went in for the idea, and 12 dummy chairs were made in Stockholm to Finn Juhl's design and placed in the mock-up that had been made of the cabin. It was naturally also Finn Juhl's hope that he would be allowed to design a more elegant chair than Douglas's rather chunky standard model. On the other hand, he realized that it would be difficult to incorporate the many technical installations without the chair's form suffering as a result. A chair of this kind had to contain a reading light, an oxygen mask, a fresh-air valve, an ash tray, a life vest, a lunch tray, etc. And everything had to be placed so practically that the passenger could reach them without any effort.

Finn Juhl never designed a chair with all these functions, since the swivel chair was abandoned and it was decided that Douglas's standard chair would be used instead. It is not clear why this decision was made. Perhaps the experiments with the mock-up in Stockholm did not go well. There were, however, at least two good reasons to give up the idea. One was the element of time: it would take time to develop a new type of chair. Finn Juhl believed that it would take at least a year. The second was safety: it was not certain that the international air carriers association would allow an arrangement by which passengers did not sit facing the front of the plane.

What remained for Finn Juhl to design were the galley, the cloak-room and lavatories, sleeping space for personnel, the lounge (for first-class passengers), and of course textiles, colors, and general lighting fixtures.

The result was a light and friendly interior characterized by Finn Juhl's bright, clear colors and good contrast tones. SAS's DC-8s were comfortable planes. Many considered them the most stylish machines in the air at the time. But unfortunately, only memories are left. DC-8s were replaced long ago by larger and more modern aircraft.

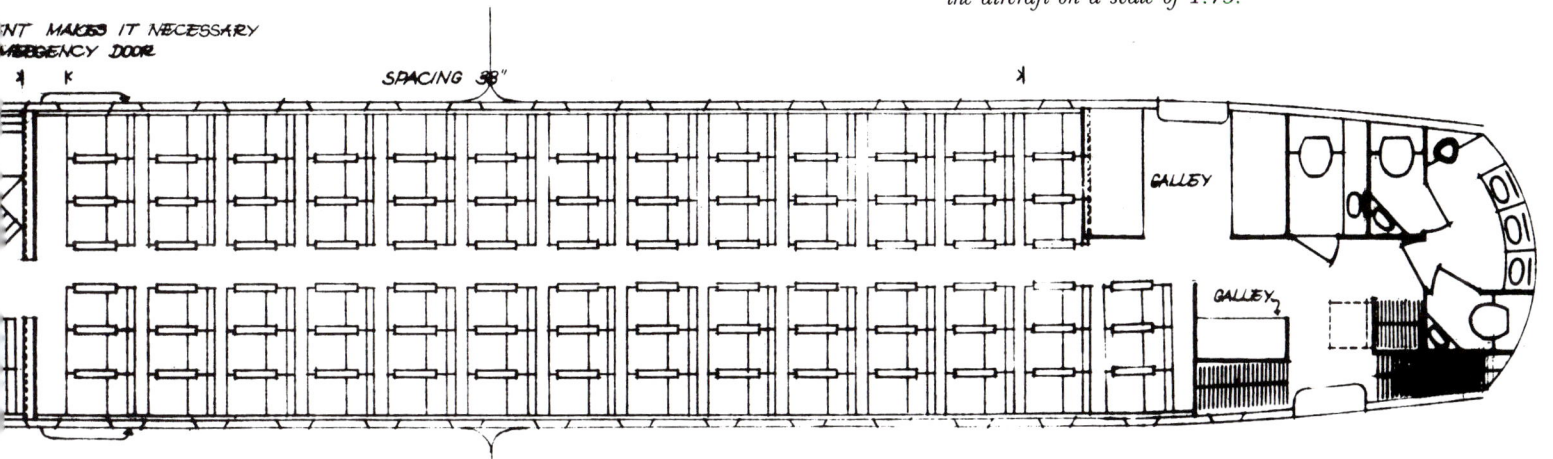

This spread: Perspective of the DC-8 cabin and floor plan of the aircraft on a scale of 1:75.

The Wilhelm Hansen store

The sheet music store at 9 Gothersgade in Copenhagen was furnished in 1916 by the architect Gotfred Tvede, who also designed the building itself. It was a fairly large room, c. 12×20 meters, with a ceiling height of about 5 meters. Tvede made two galleries, one on each side of the room, with four spiral staircases leading to them. The walls of the galleries were covered with shelves to store sheet music, and below them were bookcases.

In 1966, Finn Juhl was asked to modernized the store. The work especially involved designing new furnishings, to take the place of rather bombastic counters that took up most of the floor space, and renovating the facade. Tvede's fine galleries were not touched, except that Finn Juhl reduced the number of spiral staircases from four to two.

He designed a number of distinctive exhibition and storage counters where customers could find the sheet music they were looking for along the same principles used in modern record stores.

Since the music publisher often held receptions for large crowds in conjunction with concerts, Finn Juhl designed table tops covered with blue formica that could be put on top of the counters to have them serve as tables (at the proper height for receptions).

Finn Juhl had originally thought of using Poul Henningsen's "Artichoke" lamps for the room, but when it came down to it, he decided to keep the existing fixtures, designed by the architect Palle Suenson.

This spread: Longitudinal section of the Wilhelm Hansen store on a scale of 1:50.
Opposite page: Exhibition and storage counter on a scale of 1:20.

87

The Hotel Richmond restaurant

The restaurant that Finn Juhl was commissioned to furnish in 1965 had an entrance from the hotel lobby and was intended primarily for the hotel's guests. It was not, however, an easy task to create an intimate and cozy restaurant in this poorly proportioned room. It measured only 13 × 14 meters and had a ceiling height of 4 1/2 meters and windows on one side that stretched from floor to ceiling. Finn Juhl reduced the ceiling height to 3 1/2 meters with a dropped acoustic ceiling, and in the back part of the room he reduced it further to only 2 1/2 meters with a coffered ceiling. In the front of the room, at the same height, he suspended a lath framework which gave the appearance of taking some of the ceiling height without interfering with light from the high windows facing Vester Farimagsgade. This framework also served to conceal the electric wiring for the lamps that hung over the tables.

Part of the low area at the back of the room could be separated from the rest of the restaurant by light panels with bars so that it could be used for small parties. The panels could be slid together when they were not needed. The high part of the room in the front was separated at the middle by a wall consisting of vertical slats, which divided the room without taking daylight from the back section. In the evening, when daylight no longed played a role, the slats could be turned to create a wall separating the two rows of tables.

All of the wood used was Oregon pine. Finn Juhl also designed the rugs, brass lamps, and a completely new chair with a free arm. The arm was relatively short, so it was easy to get to and leave the tables without having to push one's chair all the way back, but long enough to provide good arm support. Finn Juhl and Niels Vodder were no longer working together at this point, so the chairs were made by the cabinetmaker L. Pontoppidan.

Here, too, as always in Finn Juhl's interiors, colors played a key role in creating the room's atmosphere. But since the restaurant was remodeled long ago, it is impossible today to describe the colors used, and Finn Juhl unfortunately left no sketches indicating them.

KELD HELMER-PETERSEN

This spread: Interior of the Hotel Richmond restaurant. Opposite page: Plan of the maximal table arrangement and ceiling plan on a scale of 1:200.

KELD HELMER-PETERSEN

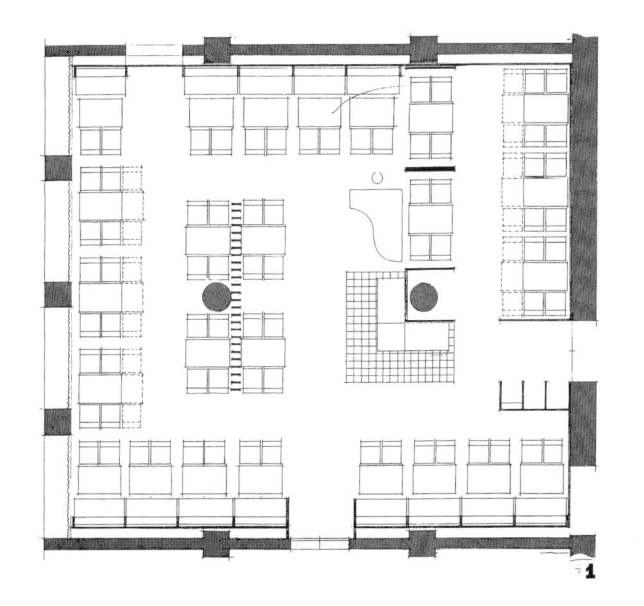

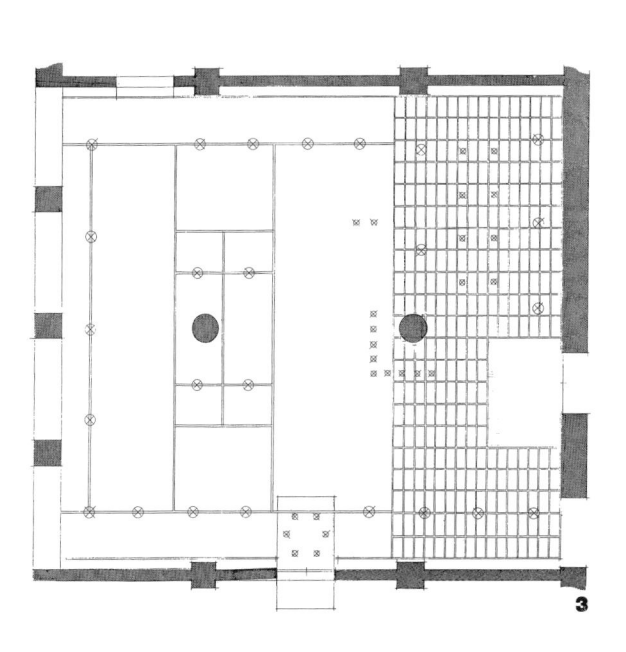

OLE WOLDBYE

HOUSES

Despite the fact that Finn Juhl had all the qualifications necessary to build fine single-family houses, and showed them with his very first house – his own – he never built more than could be counted on one hand, and even then, a couple of summer houses have to be included. He thought in rooms, which his many excellent interior designs show, and when he designed a house, he thought from the inside out. The facades were secondary; they were a function of the plan and the rooms' placement in relation to it. The rational plan, which did not take account of symmetry or other formal demands, was one of functionalism's innovations. But it naturally did not mean that the design of facades was of no importance. Facades should express the idea behind the plan and be in balance with the contrasts between wall surfaces and window sections. Finn Juhl mastered this idiom perfectly. He had an unfailing sense of how rooms would work in relation to one another, of how the effects of light in them would be, and of how the external space of the garden and the house's inner rooms would interact. His own house is a textbook example.

Finn Juhl's own house on Kratvænget

The house was built in 1942 on a magnificent site bordered on the north by the high beech trees in Ordrup Copse, on the west by Ordrupgaard Museum park, and on the south by a lower-lying residential area, with a view of Ordrup Moor. The house was placed in the northeastern corner of the site with a four-meter wide driveway along the eastern boundary.

The house consists of two parallel blocks, a short gabled house which contains the large living room and a smaller work room, and a long wing which contains the dining room, kitchen, bedrooms, and bathroom. The two blocks are linked by a lower building which holds the foyer and a room opening on to the garden. This "garden room" has an exit on the same level to the garden terrace, which lies protected in the angle between the two blocks.

The long wing is raised c. 70 cm. above the level of the living room and the "garden room," so there was space for a full cellar. This wing was later lengthened, expanding the original bedroom in the west gable into a combined living room and bedroom.

The site was originally level, but earth obtained from digging up the foundations and cellar was placed so that it took the shape of a shallow bowl, with the house lying at the bottom. The shell form first of all means that more of the lawn and low flower beds can be seen from the house than would have been possible if the site had been flat. Secondly, fairly low plants, including wild roses along the southern boundary, are enough to prevent anyone from looking in from neighboring gardens, without interfering with the view from

Finn Juhl's own house on Kratvænget seen from the boundary with Ordrupgaard.

OLE WOLDBYE

inside. And finally, it meant – an especially important feature – that the large room at the western gable of the long wing had access to the garden on the same level in spite of a 70 cm. difference in height.

The garden was designed by the garden architect Troels Erstad, who created a fine arrangement of perennials with a number of irregularly shaped beds which lie in terraces up the gentle slope in the northwestern part of the garden. An open garden pavilion was later built here.

The house is of ordinary brick which was scoured and whitewashed in a whitish-gray tone. Whitewash gives a lovely soft, mat surface, but has the disadvantage that it requires continual maintenance. Finn Juhl bitterly regretted that during his busy years he let himself be tempted by a painter's bad advice and allowed him to use plastic paint on the house. A bit of the house's original character was lost as a result.

The broad glass section (with sliding doors) in the living room was made as a construction of timber covered with Eternite in the gable. The roof is also covered with Eternite resembling light gray slate.

What especially distinguishes Finn Juhl's house is its light character, in contrast to the plants in the garden, the forest's dark, massive background, and the sharply cut, simple form of the blocks that make up the building. When snow covers the earth and plants in the

This page: The house on Kratvænget seen towards Ordrup Copse.
Opposite page: Plan on a scale of 1:100.

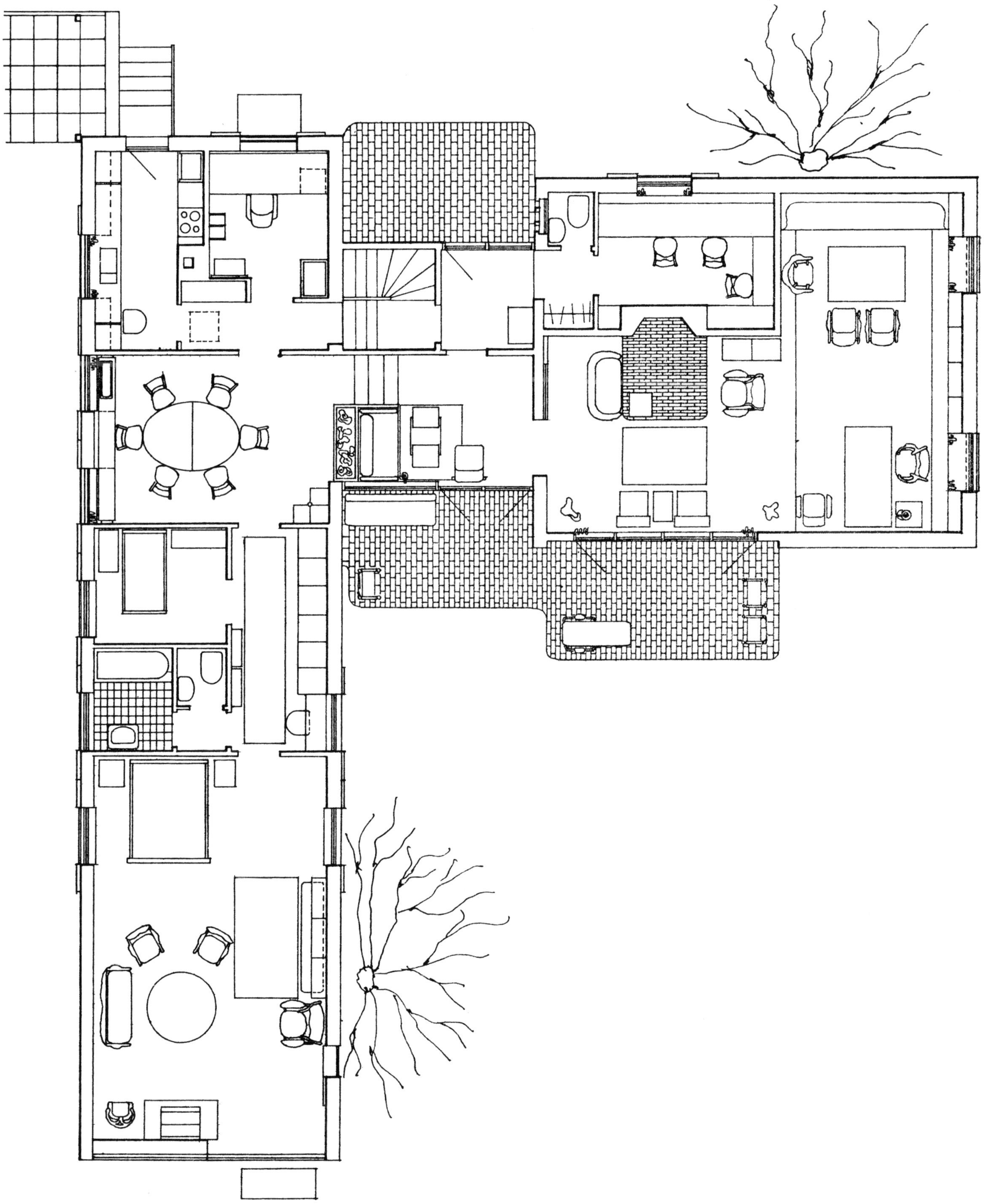

winter, it is almost like a grisaille. Finn Juhl always preferred visual lightness, and it is characteristic that he never designed a house with a blank wall or heavy tile roof, things which otherwise dominated Danish single-family housing.

The two blocks are finely balanced and clearly separated by the lower middle section, whose facade towards the garden was painted earth brown. Here, as in all Finn Juhl's work, colors play an important role, as accents and contrasts. The large awning over the glass section of the living room was curry yellow, and where the high windows reached the surface of the roof, the board above them was painted dark blue. The panel along the main door and by the glass door in the gable of the long wing was painted light blue.

The floor plan of the house is an early example of an "open plan," where the rooms have a visual transition into one another and are not, as in older houses, sharply delineated by partition walls. This principle degenerated in the course of the 1950s so that partition walls gradually disappeared almost entirely, and the kitchen ended up in the living room. In Finn Juhl's house, the principle is used in a restrained form. Each room has its clearly defined function, but no matter where one goes in the house, one has a view of the next room at all times and a glimpse of the garden as a point de vue. One visual effect is the difference in level between the two blocks, which is marked by four steps in the open link between the "garden room" and the dining room. The difference in ceiling heights also helps make the floor plan more interesting. The large living room has a slanted ceiling on two sides, one side down to a wall with bookshelves and relatively low windows. The ceilings were painted light yellow, which with the reflecting light from the garden almost looked like a tent ceiling with the light shining through.

Today it may seem a bit strange that the kitchen is so small and narrow, but here one must take into consideration that when the house was built, it was universally accepted that a rational kitchen should have the shortest possible distances between work places to save the housewife steps: it was the day of the "laboratory kitchen." Kitchens were unexplored territory in all housing construction in the 1940s. Not until the next decades did new ideas appear and fitted kitchens win the day.

When the house was built, it was a distinctive example of a modern house and garden, and with its architectonic qualities intact, it still bears excellent witness to Finn Juhl's gifts as a designer.

OLE WOLDBYE

The garden pavilion and the driveway.

95

OLE WOLDBYE

OLE WOLDBYE

This page: The living room.
Opposite page: The large room in the long wing.

OLE WOLDBYE

STRÜWING

Villa Aubertin

The house is in Rosnæs, on Nakskov Fjord, on a site that inclines slightly toward the south with a wide prospect of the fjord. The main facade is consequently turned towards the prospect and the sun. All windows face south except those in the kitchen, which nonetheless has fine southern light through a number of high windows (which do not take up wall space).

The untraditional floor plan is dominated by the large living area, which spans the south facade and consists of the gallery, on the one hand, and the dining room, which opens on the terrace, on the other.

The living room proper lies five steps lower than the dining room and is only separated from it by a few suspended shelves. It opens on a covered, sheltered area the whole breadth of the room. The large glass section has sliding doors one third of the way across. The way leading from the foyer through the dining room and living room to the terrace is, like the terrace, paved with fired brick tiles, while the floors in these two rooms and the gallery are of choice Kalmar pine. The floors in all the other rooms are covered with linoleum. The total living area is 180 sq. m.

An unusual feature of the floor plan is that the three bedrooms for the children have no windows toward the north, but instead have glass doors and windows on the gallery. In this way these rooms also have the view and, like the kitchen, receive fine southern light through the highly placed windows. They have only a porthole on the northern side.

The client, the lumber dealer M. Aubertin, and his wife, were great admirers of Finn Juhl, so they wanted his furniture for their house and also let him design all the built-in fixtures.

Opposite page: Villa Aubertin, built in 1952, seen from the south. The recessed building on the left houses a hobby room, guest room, etc.
This page: The plan on a scale of 1:125.

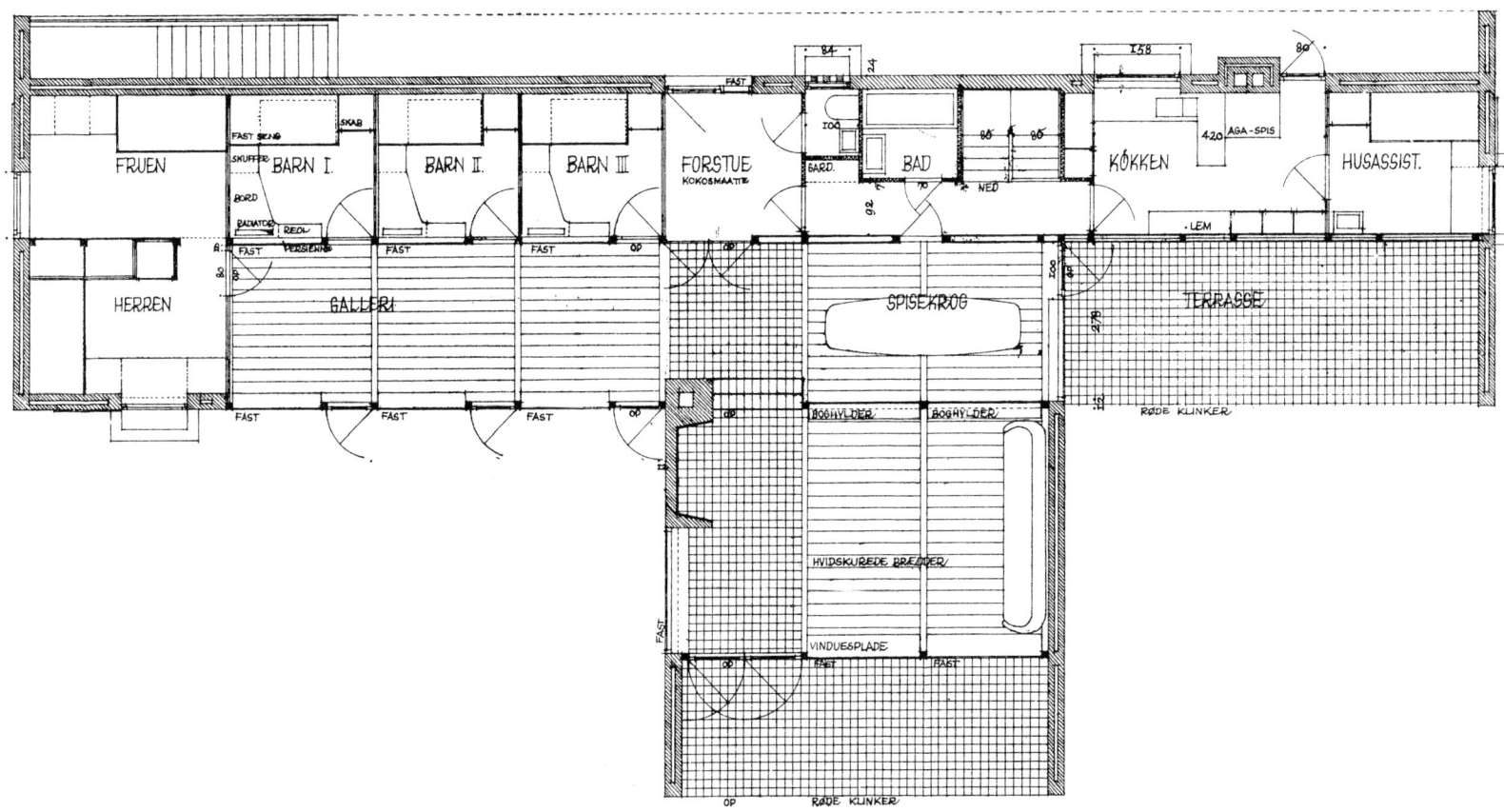

ERIK HANSEN

ERIK HANSEN

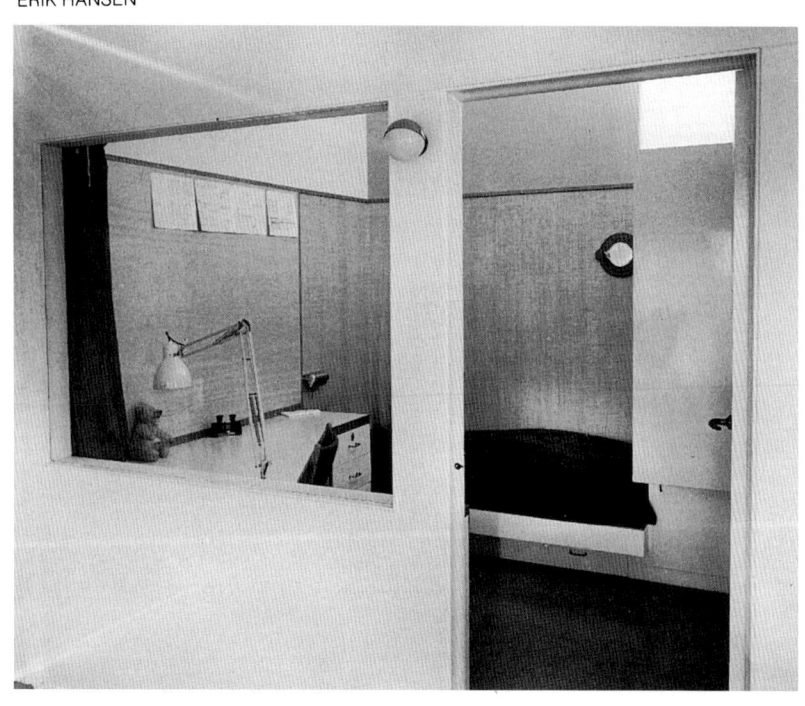

Above, the dining room opening on the terrace. Below, one of the small rooms with glass partitions towards the gallery.

STRÜWING

ERIK HANSEN

Above, the living room with hanging shelves seen facing the dining room. Below, the gallery with windows facing south and glass partitions between it and the small bedrooms.

STRÜWING

Summer house in Asserbo

The house was built in 1950 for Mrs. Anthon Petersen on a scenic untouched site on Nyvej in Asserbo. The floor plan, as always in Finn Juhl's houses, is clear and carefully conceived. A long, low wing which contains the foyer, kitchen, utility room, children's room, guest room, maid's room, and carport faces north. The large living room, which faces on a covered terrace, Mrs. Petersen's own bedroom, and a second guest room face south. The living room is high with uncovered rafters. In addition to light from the terrace doors and a couple of large windows facing east, it receives light from a number of highly placed windows facing north. As a result, the slanted ceiling is always evenly illuminated during the day, which helps make the room, paneled with birch veneer, appear light and airy. The large fireplace is double-sided, making it possible to heat it up both from the living room and from the covered terrace. The house is made completely of wood, with horizontal tarred cladding.

This page: Above, the entrance. Below, the covered terrace and an isometric drawing showing the division into a low wing and a high block with roof sloping on one side.
Opposite page: The facade towards the south and the plan on a scale of 1:125.

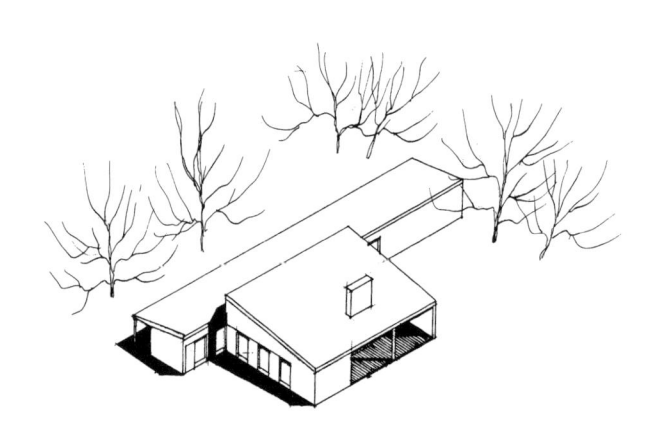

STRÜWING

103

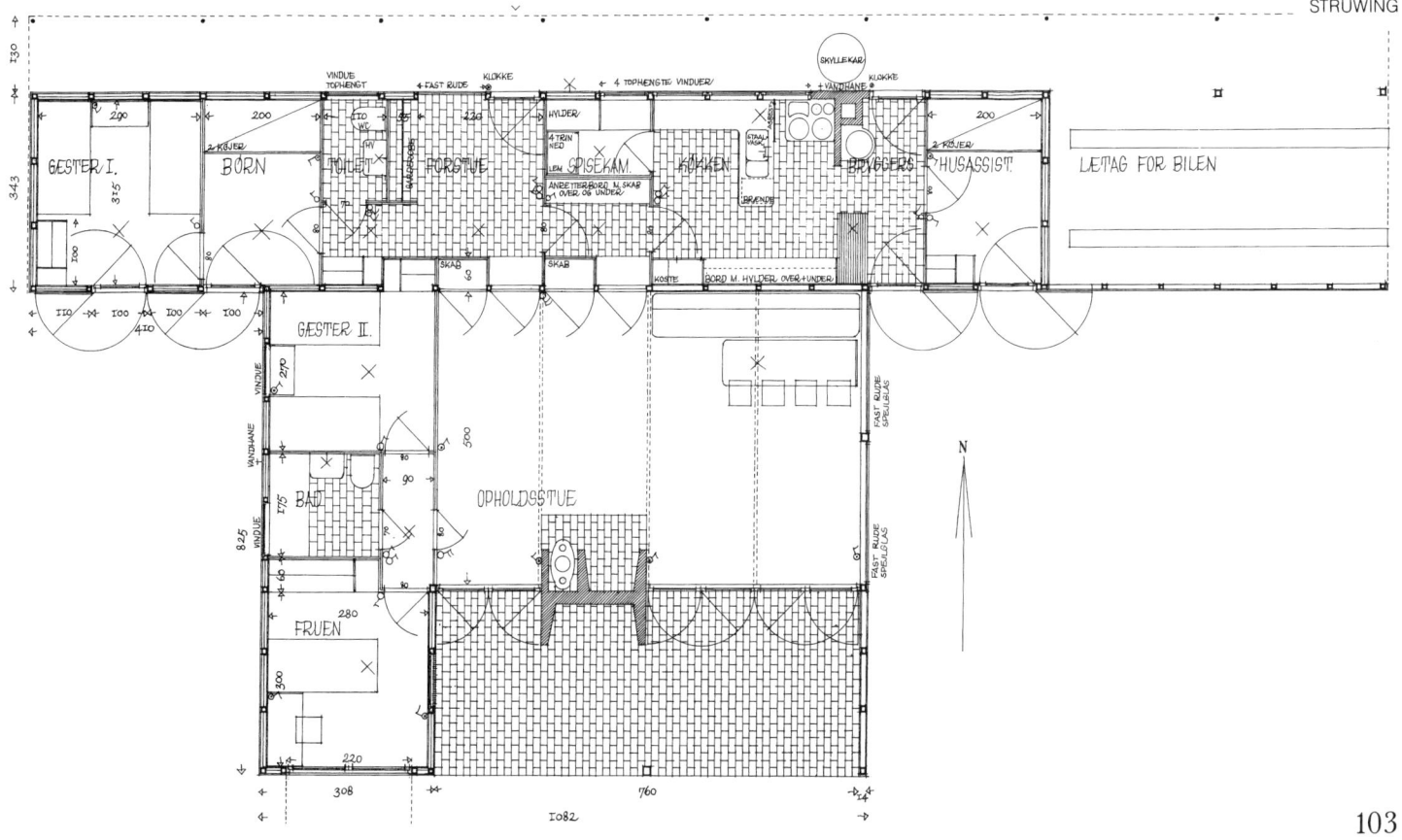

Summer house in Raageleje

This house was built in 1962 for Anders Hostrup-Petersen. Outwardly, it is a modest house, which blends in as much as possible with the beautiful landscape. The gable on the north, which is lengthened into a windbreak, is made of light cement blocks, but otherwise the house is constructed of wood, with narrow vertical cladding. The floor plan of this house, too, is clear and simple. Between the large living room and the sleeping area is a dining room opening on to the kitchen, which is very small. Both the dining room and the living room have access to the covered terrace. The sleeping area has its own entrance from a covered porch.

The kitchen proved too small in practice, so that a larger one was later added on outside the living room and original kitchen, which was then used as a butler's pantry. The addition also made it possible to place the entrance to the cellar in the kitchen.

While the house was simple and unpretentious on the outside, it was very finely conceived inside, using exquisite materials. The house was furnished largely with Finn Juhl's own furniture.

KELD HELMER-PETERSEN

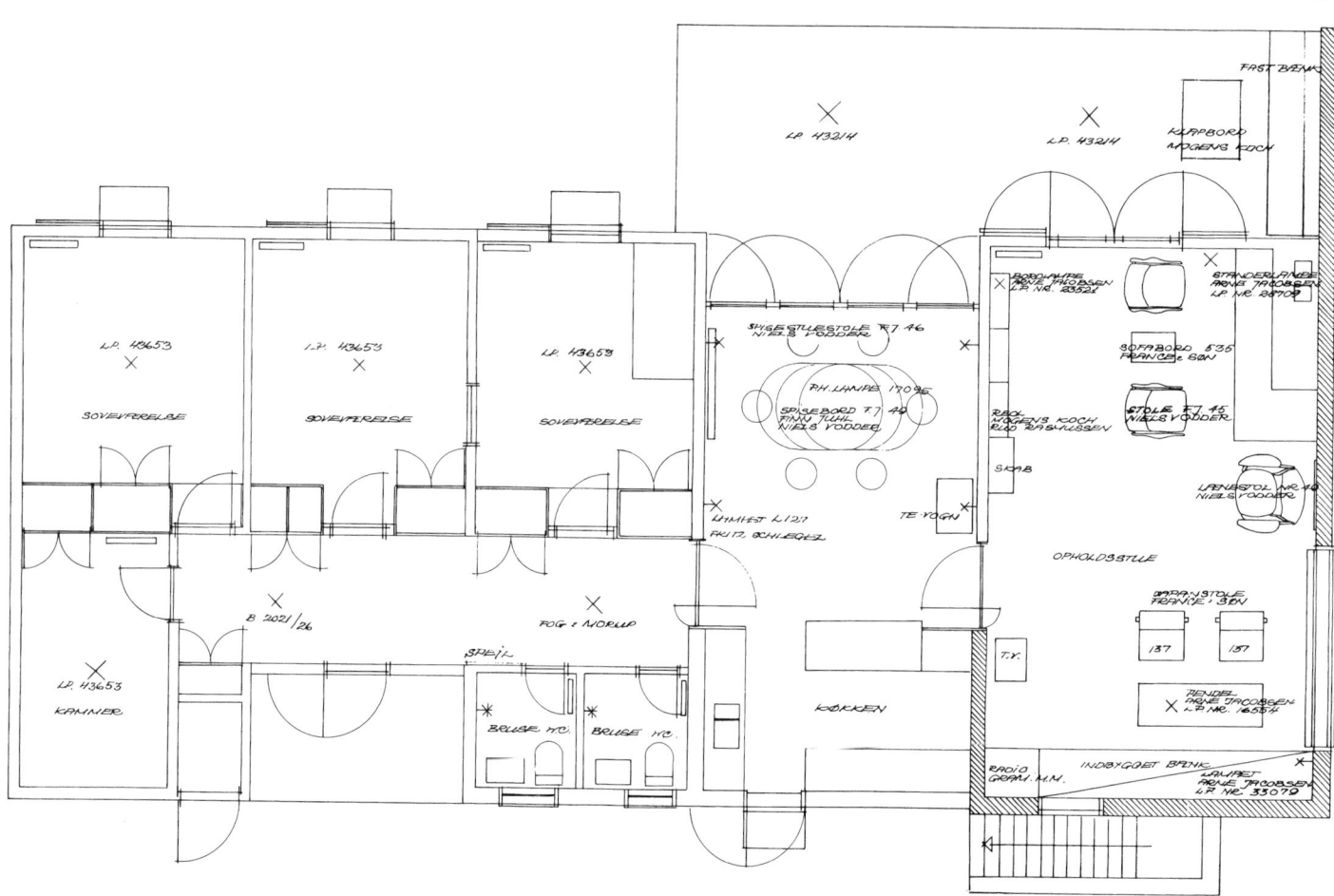

KELD HELMER-PETERSEN

KELD HELMER-PETERSEN

Opposite page: The house seen from the northwest and the covered terrace, and a plan on a scale of 1:100.
This page: Above, the dining area seen from the terrace; in the middle, the same area seen from the kitchen; and below, the room with fireplace and Finn Juhl's furniture. The painting is by Vilhelm Lundstrøm.

Project for two houses in Klelund

Finn Juhl designed a distinctive plan for two houses in Klelund, in Jutland, for Count L.N. Moltke-Huitfeld. The plan for one house actually involved remodeling an existing building, which lay on a hilly area adjoining a fish farm. The other was for a completely new single-family house linked to the existing building.

The two houses, which would have had an excellent view of the river valley, were to be reached from the north, and Finn Juhl designed a joint courtyard which was to be enclosed on the south by a low wall linking the two houses.

In the plan, the existing house was changed and expanded so radically that one would hardly believe that it was an old building. The rooms were placed around a room with a fireplace which, like the living room and dining room, had direct access to a large terrace on the south.

The new house, located east of the existing building in the plan, also had a room with a fireplace facing south and access from it to

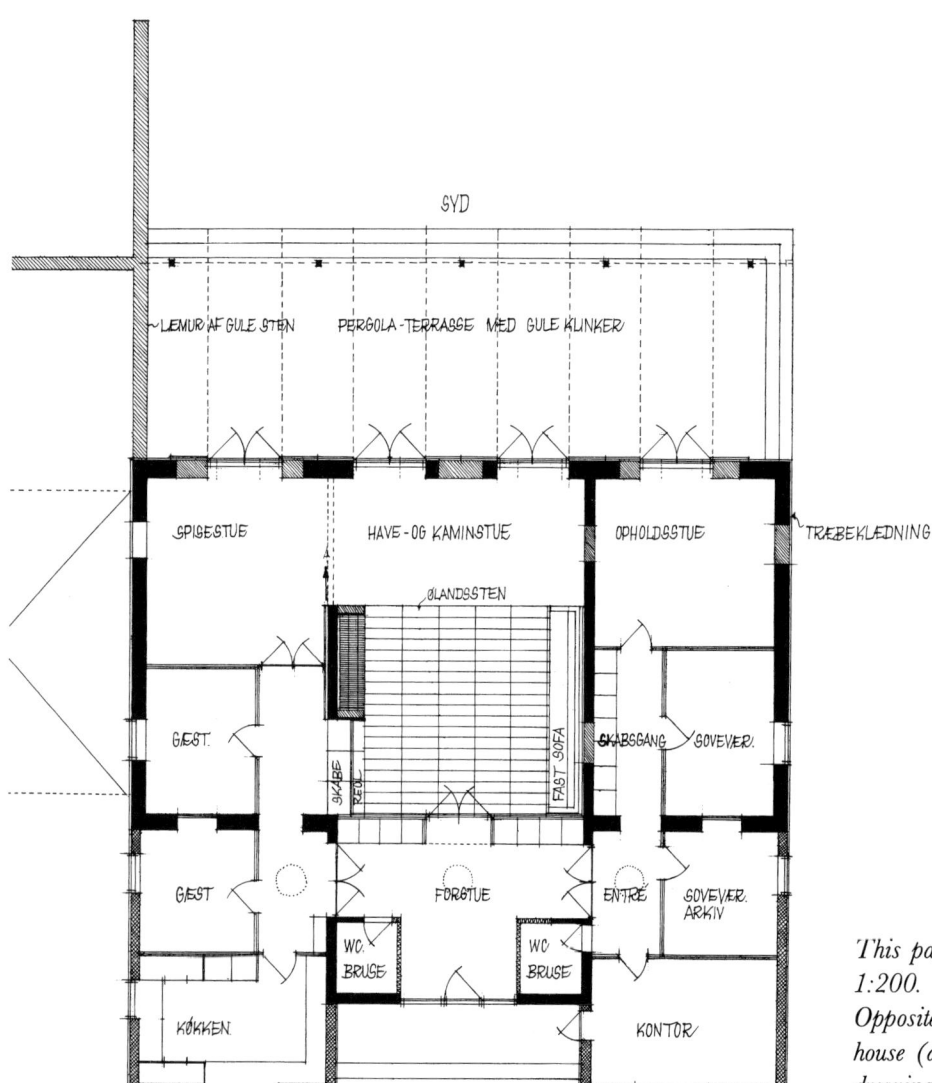

This page: Plan of the house to be remodeled, on a scale of 1:200.

Opposite page: Drawing showing a cross section of the new house (above), a general plan (middle), and an isometric drawing of the whole area (below).

107

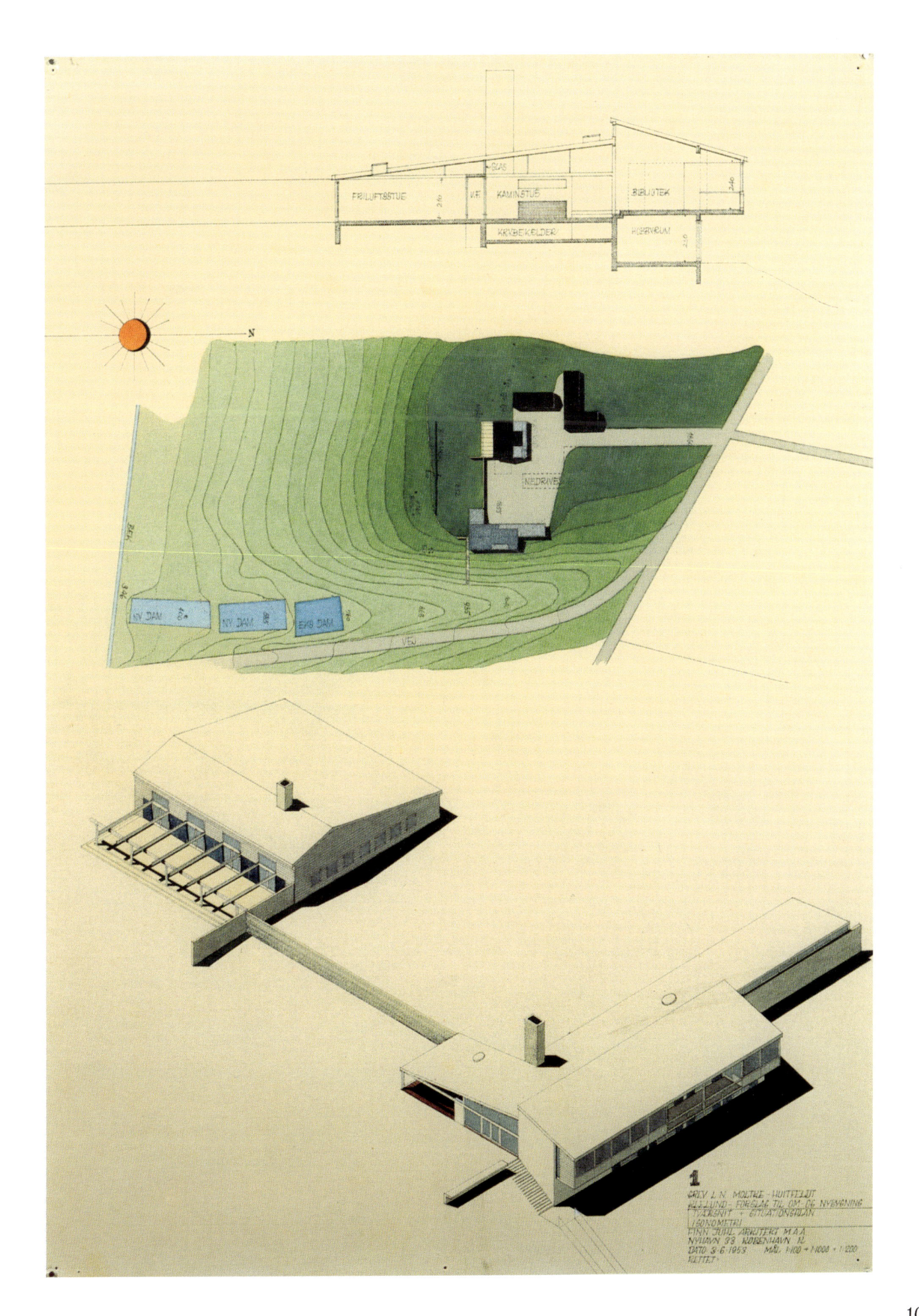

108

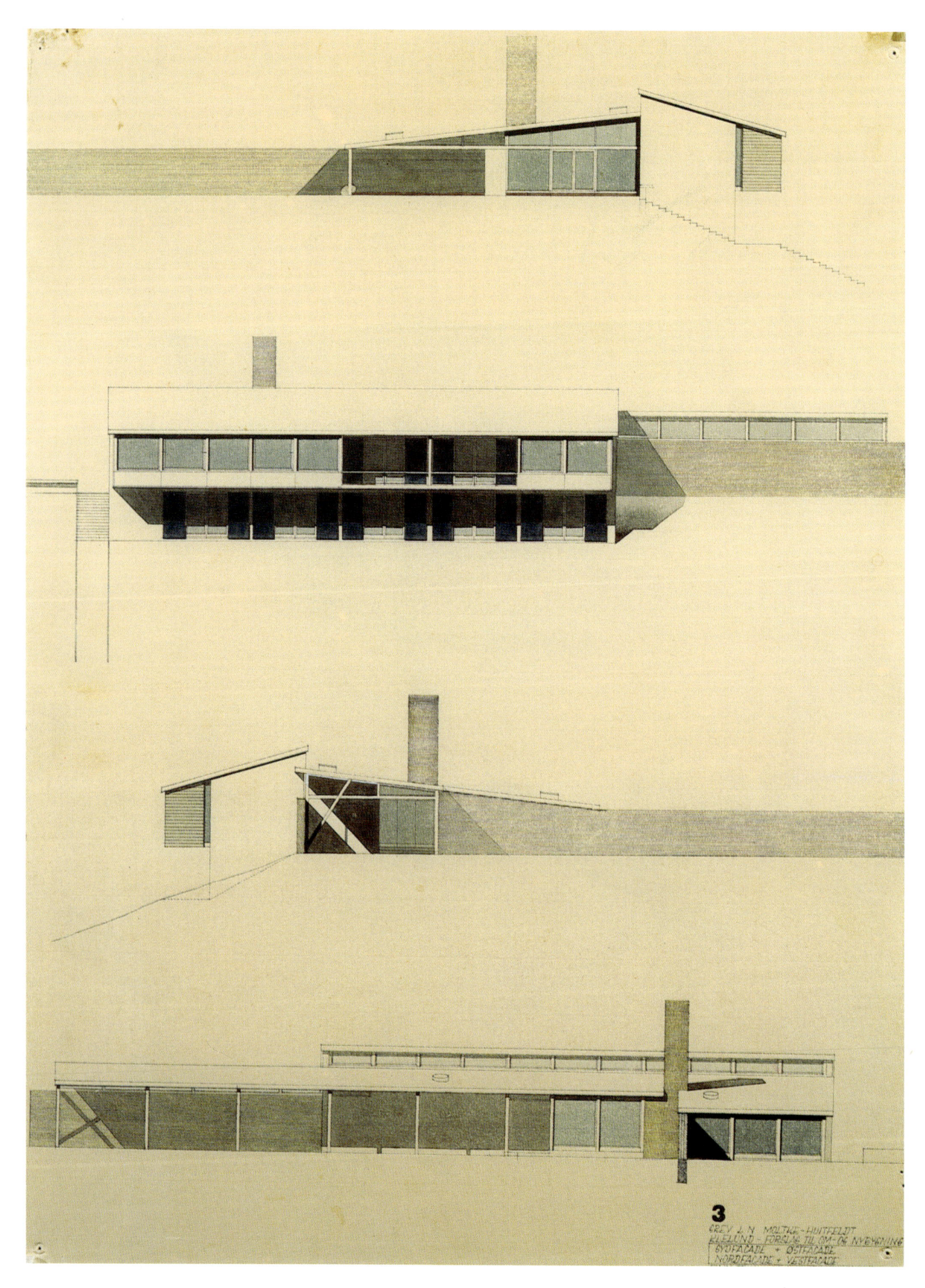

Opposite page: Section and facades of the new house.
This page: Plan of the new house on a scale of 1:200.

a covered terrace facing the same direction. The large living room, adjacent to the room with a fireplace, faced east, as did the kitchen and sleeping quarters. Advantage was taken of the sharply sloping site so that the cellar storey, which also contained a hobby room, could comprise a full storey with doors facing east.

The project, which was not carried out, shows Finn Juhl's ability to exploit all the potentials that hilly terrain offers and to create vital, exciting architecture. In this project he worked in the best functionalist tradition, where the main disposition of the floor plan is clearly expressed in the facades, and where the individual blocks of the house and roof surfaces intersect in a harmonious way.

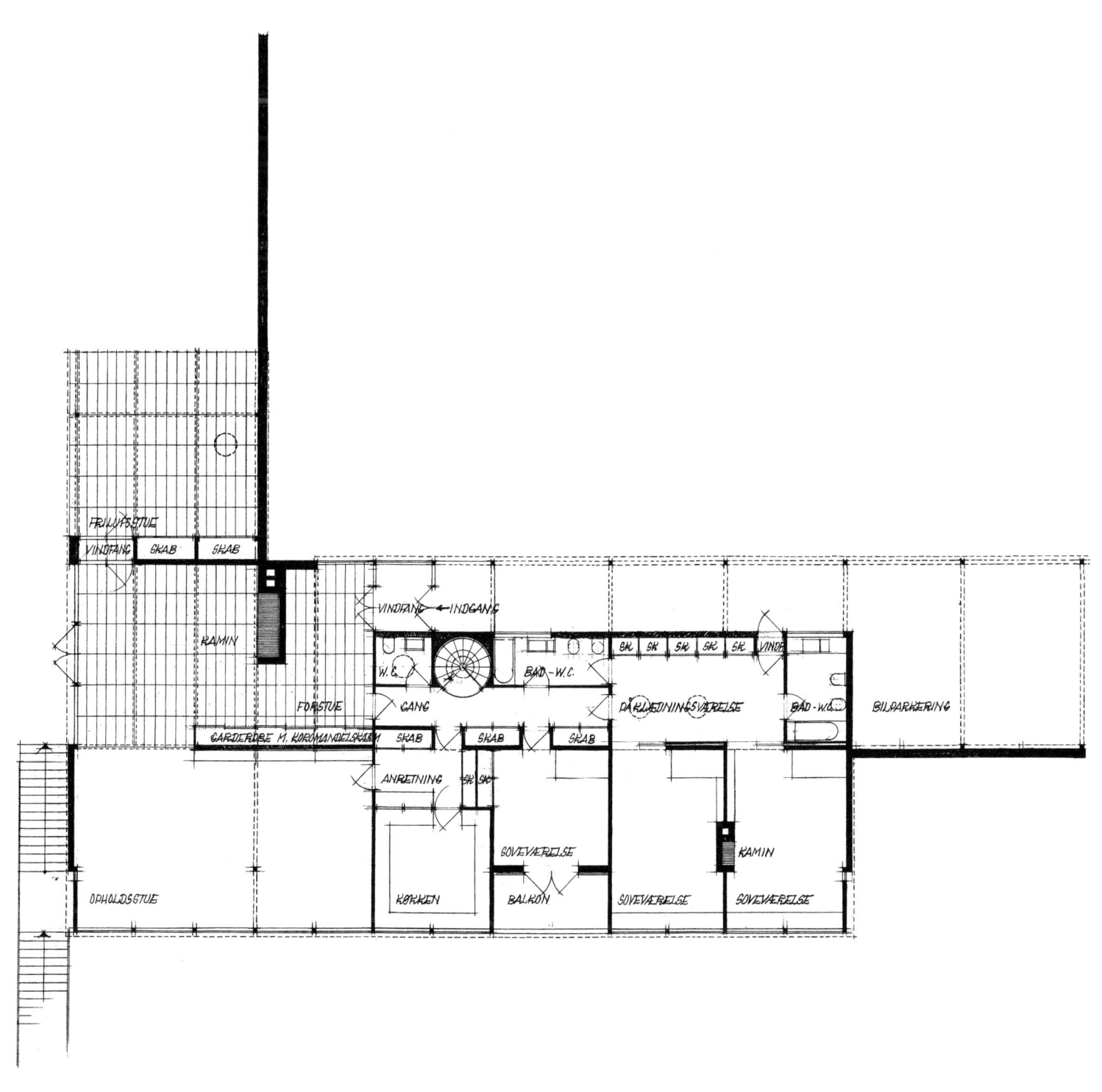

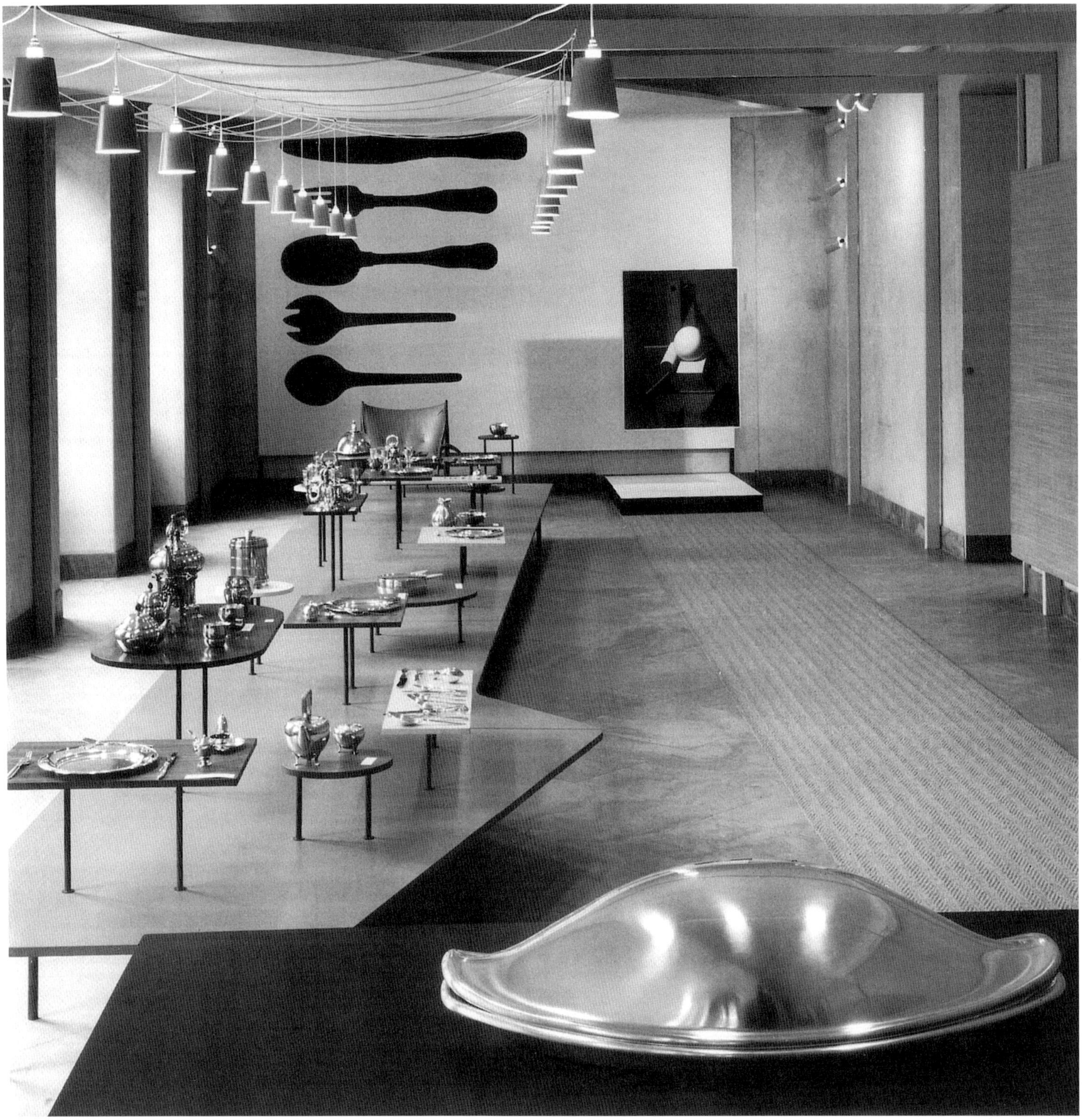

EXHIBITIONS

Designing exhibitions of arts and crafts and decorative art requires improvisation – but carefully planned improvisation. This may sound like a paradox, but the truth is that though an exhibition must be worked out on the drawing board and prepared down to the last detail, it takes its final form on the spot. The task is – often with very short notice – to create space, light, and atmosphere around the objects to be exhibited, to emphasize their uniqueness. A framework must be created, but it must not be anonymous, and neither must it be so obtrusive that it steals the viewer's interest from the objects that are, after all, the exhibition's *raison d'être*. The rooms made available for exhibitions are often highly unsuitable for the intimate interplay that an exhibition of arts and crafts is, and the exhibition architect is often bound by financial and other constraints that it can be necessary to break if artistic harmony is to emerge from the exhibition as a whole.

Finn Juhl mastered the art of creating an exhibition so that the objects presented came into their own. Bent Salicath gave a highly picturesque description of the way Finn Juhl worked when he arranged an exhibition: "...As an exhibition man, Finn Juhl also worked with acute awareness of spacial effects. The precision and good layout were obvious, along with a musicality of color in his display. Something that was not easy became a ballet. – Finn Juhl's sketches were clearly painted works which denoted a rhythm and an almost fragrant curiosity about how the exhibitions that he was designing would eventually present themselves. – When he stands on the spot and is to set things up, he has almost a conductor's disappointed movements in his facial expression, imperious miens, and finally a little ironic laughter, which almost always hangs down at the corner of his mouth together with a cigarette, like a relaxed conductor's baton. – As he sets things up, one once again notices the sensitive hands which know what they want, but which also want to improvise. When an exhibition finally stands there, it does not interest him a whit. The performance is finished. The orchestra can go home."[15]

Georg Jensen anniversary exhibition

In 1954, 50 years had passed since the sculptor and silversmith Georg Jensen established his modest workshop in Copenhagen behind the gateway at 36 Bredgade. In time he became one of the few Danish craftsmen to win world renown. The reason for his success was first and foremost that he was an original and self-confident artist. But if a little workshop is able to grow to become one of Denmark's largest decorative arts enterprises, many other factors are naturally involved. One of them was that the silversmithy took pains

Opposite page: Interior from the Georg Jensen anniversary exhibition at the Museum of Decorative Art in 1954. In the foreground, Henning Koppel's large covered fish platter. The painting is by Vilhelm Lundstrøm.

112

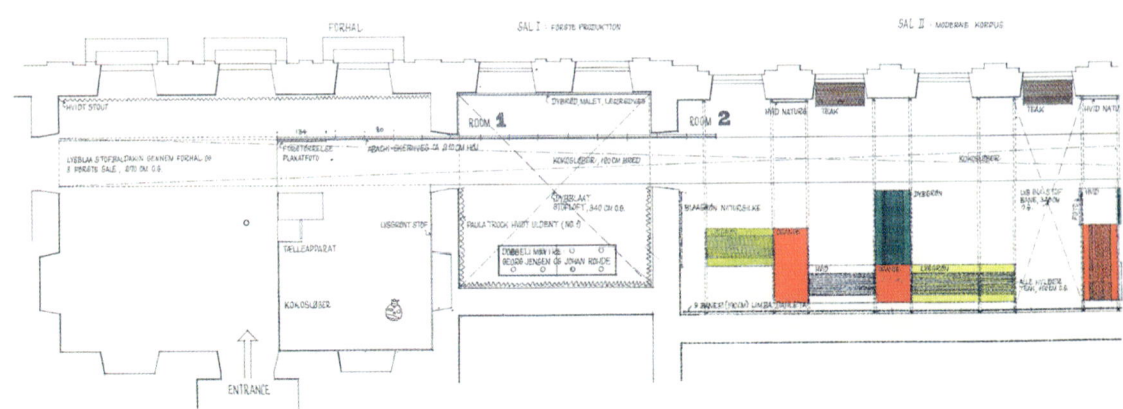

This spread: Plan of the exhibition on a scale of 1:200. Opposite page: Interior of the exhibition. A complete set of Johan Rohde's "Acorn" silverware was exhibited on the round table. It was designed in 1915 and is still produced.
This page: Interior of the exhibition with Henning Koppel's covered fish platter and pitcher.

to participate in the many international exhibitions, including world expositions. It was through these exhibitions that Georg Jensen became internationally famous, and this was the reason for the company's exports, which grew considerably over the years. It consequently almost became a rule that the smithy's success was to be cemented and new triumphs won through exhibitions.

After the First World War, in 1920, the smithy held its first major exhibition in Denmark. The whole Charlottenborg exhibition building had been rented, and the event was a tremendous success. For the first time, the Danes truly realized how nationally significant the Georg Jensen silversmithy had become.

Throughout the 1930s, the company's activities were based largely on exports. Consequently, the Second World War and the German occupation of Denmark naturally created major problems. When the smithy celebrated its 50th anniversary in 1954, however, it was in the midst of a new period of expansion, both artistically and commercially. This is why the company wanted to mark its anniversary with a new important exhibition, and the job of designing it was given to Finn Juhl. It was his first large-scale exhibition commission in Denmark, and he carried it out with mastery.

The exhibition was held at the Museum of Decorative Art. The museum's rooms are very cool, with floors of gray marble flagging and gray-plastered walls that reflect very little light, so they were in themselves an impossible background for silver. Finn Juhl created a flattering background by covering the walls with lengths of woven bast or cloth in different harmonizing colors, and the whole exhibition, which occupied many rooms, was given cohesion by light canopies of cloth that, together with cocoanut mat runners on the floor,

113

This page: Interior of the exhibition "50 Years of Danish Silver" at the Speed Museum in Louisville, Kentucky.
Opposite page: Above, an interior of the exhibition at the Corcoran Museum in Washington, D.C., and below, at the Virginia Museum of Fine Arts in Richmond.

marked the visitors' progress from room to room. The objects were exhibited on panels covered with palisander veneer or painted mat black which were separated from the gray floors by other panels painted different colors. Only jewelry and other small objects were exhibited in showcases. The overall impression of the exhibition was of lightness and elegance.

The exhibition was later – in slightly reduced form – moved to London and then to the United States, where it was shown under the title of "50 Years of Danish Silver" at the Corcoran Museum in Washington, D.C., the Speed Museum in Louisville, Kentucky, and the Dallas Museum of Fine Arts in Texas in 1955, at the Virginia Museum of Fine Arts in Richmond in 1956, and at the City Art Museum in Saint Louis, Missouri, in 1957. Finn Juhl had to design a new exhibition lay-out for each museum, since the rooms that were made available were naturally highly diverse.

"Home of the Future" at Forum

It is almost obligatory for every major exhibition of modern living to have a "Home of the Future" as a special attraction. And who would not like to see into the future? When the Copenhagen Cabinetmakers' Guild held a large exhibition at the Forum exhibition center in 1954 to celebrate its 400th anniversary, Finn Juhl was asked to design a home of the future. Precisely during this period, experimentation was going on both in Denmark and abroad with single-family houses with "open plans," which were to make houses more interesting and promote more informal living. This was considered the type of housing that would be used in the future, so it was natural for Finn Juhl to give his version.

The house was divided into two sections by a little atrium, or walled-in garden. On the left was the living room, with access to the kitchen and dining area and an exit to the terrace (visitors had to imagine the sliding doors). On the right were the sleeping and recreational areas, with access through a hall with closets.

Built-in units were used extensively for furnishings. This was true not only of closets, but also of work tables in the hobby and play room, the long bench in the dining area, the wall of closets between the kitchen and the living room, which held radio and TV, etc., and finally the long sofa by the fireplace.

Even though Finn Juhl in principle designed an open plan, he did think that it should be possible to separate the different sections and rooms with sliding doors, so that the members of the family could have the privacy they wish.

STRÜWING

This page: "Home of the Future" at the Cabinetmakers' Guild anniversary exhibition at the Forum exhibition hall in 1954. The kitchen with the dining area seen from the atrium. The sculpture in the foreground is by Erik Thommesen. As a point de vue for the hall on the right is Henrik Starcke's model for the figure in the Trusteeship Council Chamber at the U.N. (see page 76).
Opposite page: Interior with the long bench used for sitting and working. Plan on a scale of 1:125.

STRÜWING

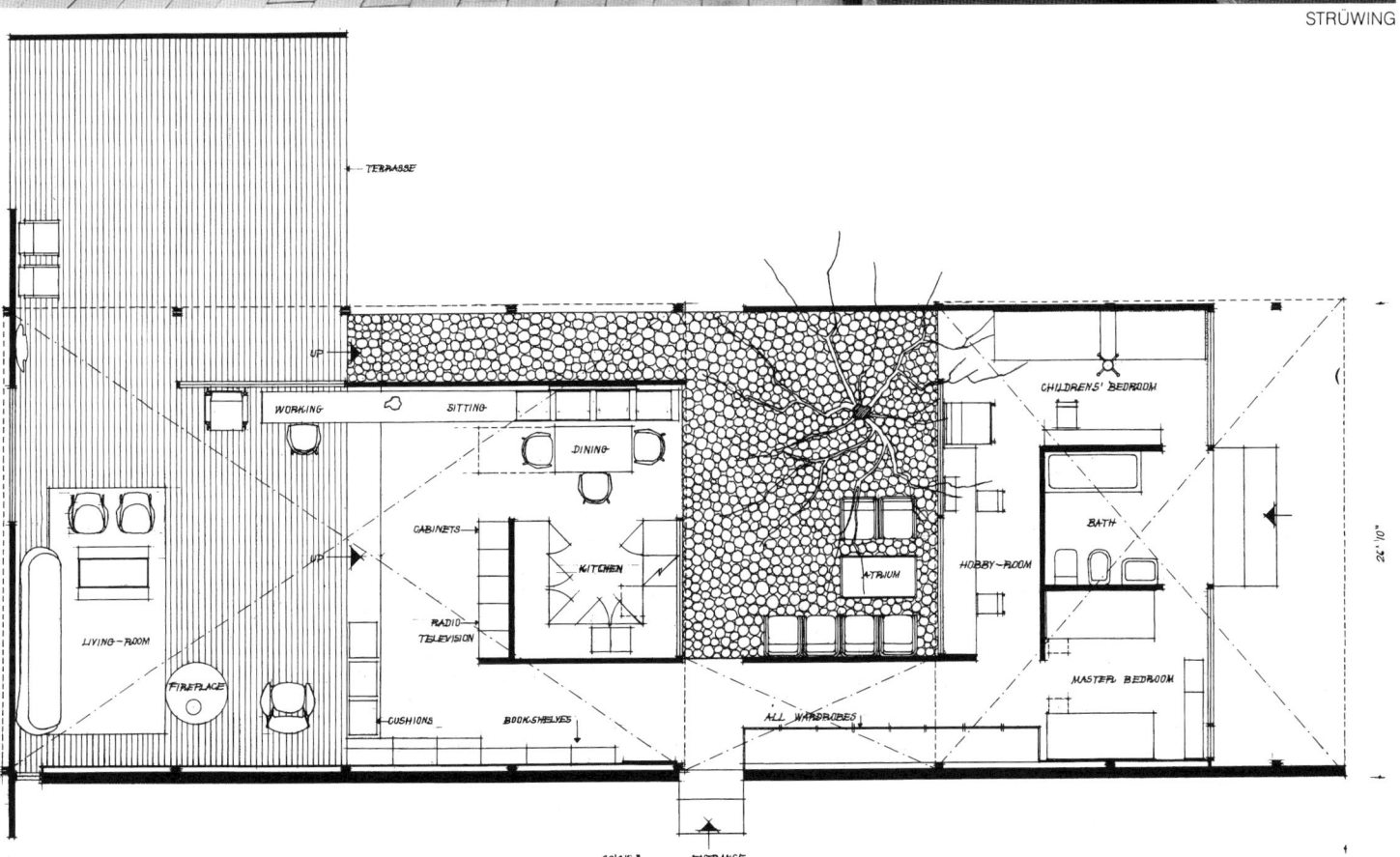

117

"The Arts of Denmark" in New York

The exhibition that was shown at the Metropolitan Museum of Art in New York was the most ambitious exhibition project ever launched by the Danish Society of Arts and Crafts. Since the exhibition was part of a large-scale Danish campaign in the United States, it was an official function, with King Frederik IX and President Eisenhower as patrons. The Society had originally wanted an exhibition of modern Danish applied art, but the museum, one of the world's most distinguished, only wanted to take an exhibition that showed Danish applied art throughout the ages – and this wish had to be respected. The Exhibition was given the subtitle "Viking to Modern," but it actually went even farther back in time, since it began with examples of utilitarian objects from the Stone Age – flint knives, arrow heads, etc.

As a result, modern arts and crafts took up only a small part of the otherwise very large exhibition area that was made available, and Finn Juhl's task as exhibition architect was therefore actually to arrange a museum showing. It was impossible to build up any real framework. Luckily, the exhibition rooms were sober and well lighted, and so this was not really necessary. Finn Juhl consequently chose to link the individual rooms with light canopies and in other ways let the objects appeal to the viewer through the effects of their own colors and materials.

Great pains had been taken to choose things from the different historical periods that corresponded to our own time's conceptions of quality – objects with simple forms and a refined or bold use of materials. Even if it is probably a form of falsification of history to present such a harmonious picture of Danish applied art throughout the ages, the exhibition, under Finn Juhl's capable hands, had a unique uniformity, and was a great success.

BENTE HAMANN

This spread: Interiors from "The Arts of Denmark" at the Metropolitan Museum of Art in New York in 1960.

BENTE HAMANN

BENTE HAMANN

119

"Two Centuries of Danish Design" in London

The next major official exhibition that Finn Juhl designed was "Two Centuries of Danish Design" at the Victoria & Albert Museum in London in 1968. This exhibition, too, was part of a large-scale PR campaign for Denmark in England and Scotland, so King Frederik and Queen Elizabeth were its patrons.

As had been the case in New York, the Society had wished to present an exhibition of only modern arts and crafts, but the museum wanted a historical element if it was to take the exhibition at all. This time it was not necessary to go all the way back to the Stone Age, however. The museum was satisfied with an introduction consisting of examples of art and applied art from the latter half of the 18th century and the 19th century. Especially silver, porcelain, and furniture were chosen.

In contrast to the exhibition rooms at the Metropolitan, the rooms that were put at the exhibition's disposal at the Victoria & Albert were to say the least unsuited to an intimate presentation of refined applied art. They had no natural lighting, and the ceilings were over five meters high. Finn Juhl had originally thought of designing special exhibition displays for the occasion, but when he saw the rooms, he realized that the money available had to be used to completely eliminate the awful surroundings. And so he decided to use the Abstracta system of showcases and tables designed by Poul Cadovius and to cover the large exhibition area completely with unbleached canvas. The Abstracta system is exceedingly flexible and

The exhibition "Two Centuries of Danish Design" at the Victoria & Albert Museum in London in 1968. The foyer and examples of furniture and arts and crafts from the 18th and 19th centuries seen from the entrance. The canopy led the visitor into the large exhibition room on the left of the foyer.

EDGAR HYMANN

Interiors of the exhibition in the large room with applied art from our own century. The lower picture shows the canopy that linked the foyer with the large room. Købke's portrait of the sculptor H.E. Freund is the point de vue.

EDGAR HYMANN

made it possible to create a room within a room, so to speak.

In addition to the large exhibition room, there was a foyer providing access to it from the side. Finn Juhl used this foyer as an introduction to the older arts and crafts, and from it he ran a canopy into the large room, guiding the public to it in a natural way. All in all, he was able to create a harmonious exhibition.

EDGAR HYMANN

After London, the exhibition was moved the same year to Glasgow, and then to Manchester. In Glasgow, it was set up at the Kelvingrove Museum, a bombastic building from Victorian times. It is a museum with highly diverse collections. It is an art museum (with a very fine art collection), a zoological museum, a local history museum, a technical museum, and much more. From the gigantic foyer one saw in the room on the left an enormous model of the Atlantic liner Queen Elizabeth 2, which had been built in Glasgow, and in the room on the right a stuffed giraffe! The exhibition was to be mounted in this foyer: not an easy task. Finn Juhl once again made a room within a room, but he had to give up the idea of covering it, among other things because all daylight came from the foyer's skylights.

In Manchester, the exhibition was shown at the Whitworth Art Gallery, a fine little museum which belongs to Manchester University. In contrast to the Victoria & Albert and Kelvingrove, this museum had very fine and suitable rooms for changing exhibitions. They were both well lighted and made of very high quality materials, something that admirably suited the exhibition's refined applied arts. Of the three exhibitions, this was decidedly the most beautiful.

The version of the exhibition shown in Glasgow and Manchester was titled "A Century of Danish Design," since it only included applied art from our own century.

"A Century of Danish Design" in the large middle hall of the Kelvingrove Museum in Glasgow.

ELSAM, MANN & COOPER

ELSAM, MANN & COOPER

"A Century of Danish Design" at the Whitworth Art Gallery in Manchester.

123

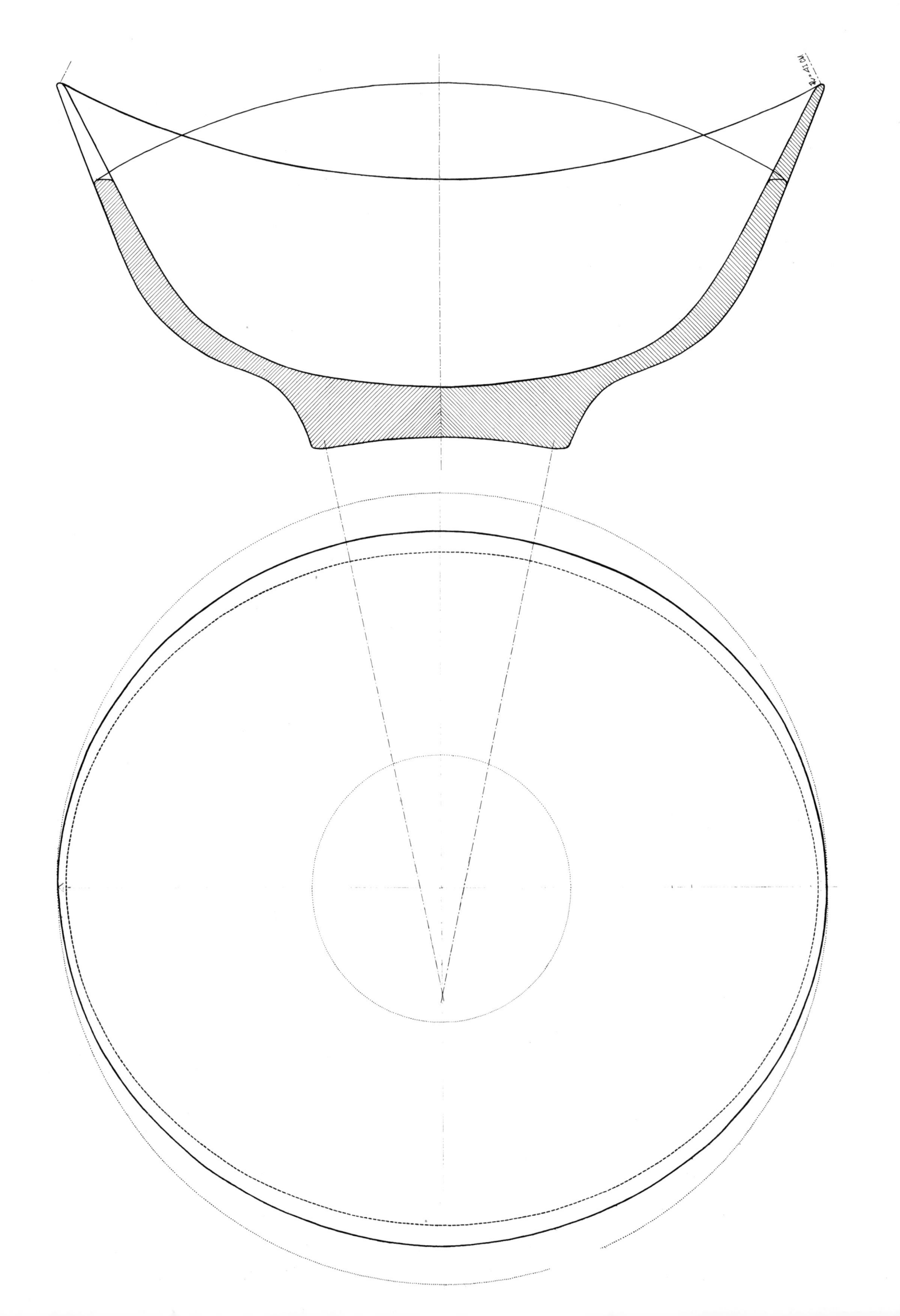

APPLIED ART

In 1950, Finn Juhl wrote this confession: "Paradoxically, one can say that if I manage before I take my leave of this world to fill the house I have designed with furniture, rugs, curtains, fittings, table services, glass, silver, etc. that I myself have designed, then I will have reached my true goal."[16]

He did reach this goal as far as furniture is concerned, but had difficulty with the other items. The year he wrote this, he was full of optimism, since his drawing board was stacked with commissions. Just then he was working on a service for Bing & Grøndahl, which wanted to launch it in connection with its centenary in 1953. Even though models were made of several parts of the service, it was abandoned, but it is not known why. Perhaps there was too little time available for a factory to produce a new porcelain service; perhaps Finn Juhl's forms were not distinctive enough to guarantee market success. No matter the reason, the project was abandoned and Finn Juhl was greatly disappointed.

At about the same time, he took part in a competition for silver flatware announced by Georg Jensen, but he did not win a prize. These two disappointments probably took some of his courage, since he never again attempted to design porcelain or silver.

Many years after, in 1969, he had contacts with the famous Venini glassworks in Murano, and the designs he left include several for glass. Apparently none of these designs was produced, either.

It is regrettable that Finn Juhl never had the opportunity to design things in porcelain, silver, and glass since his excellent abilities as a designer can be seen quite clearly in the series of wooden bowls that he created for Kay Bojesen in 1951 and 1954. The large bowl, especially, is still a distinctive and timeless creation.

Opposite page: Drawing for the large salad bowl that Finn Juhl designed for Kay Bojesen Modeller in 1951, here shown on a scale of 1:2.

Three bowls made of teak by the skilled turner Magne Monsen, who worked for Kay Bojesen Modeller.

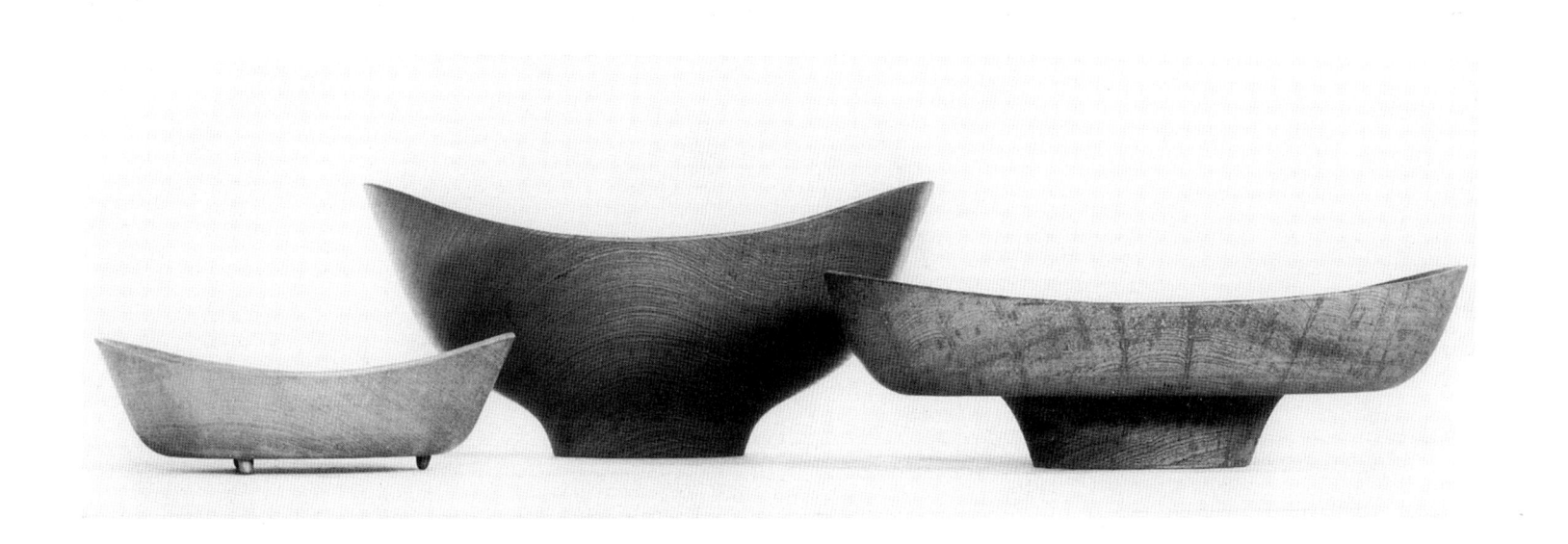

APERTO   CHIARO — BIANCO

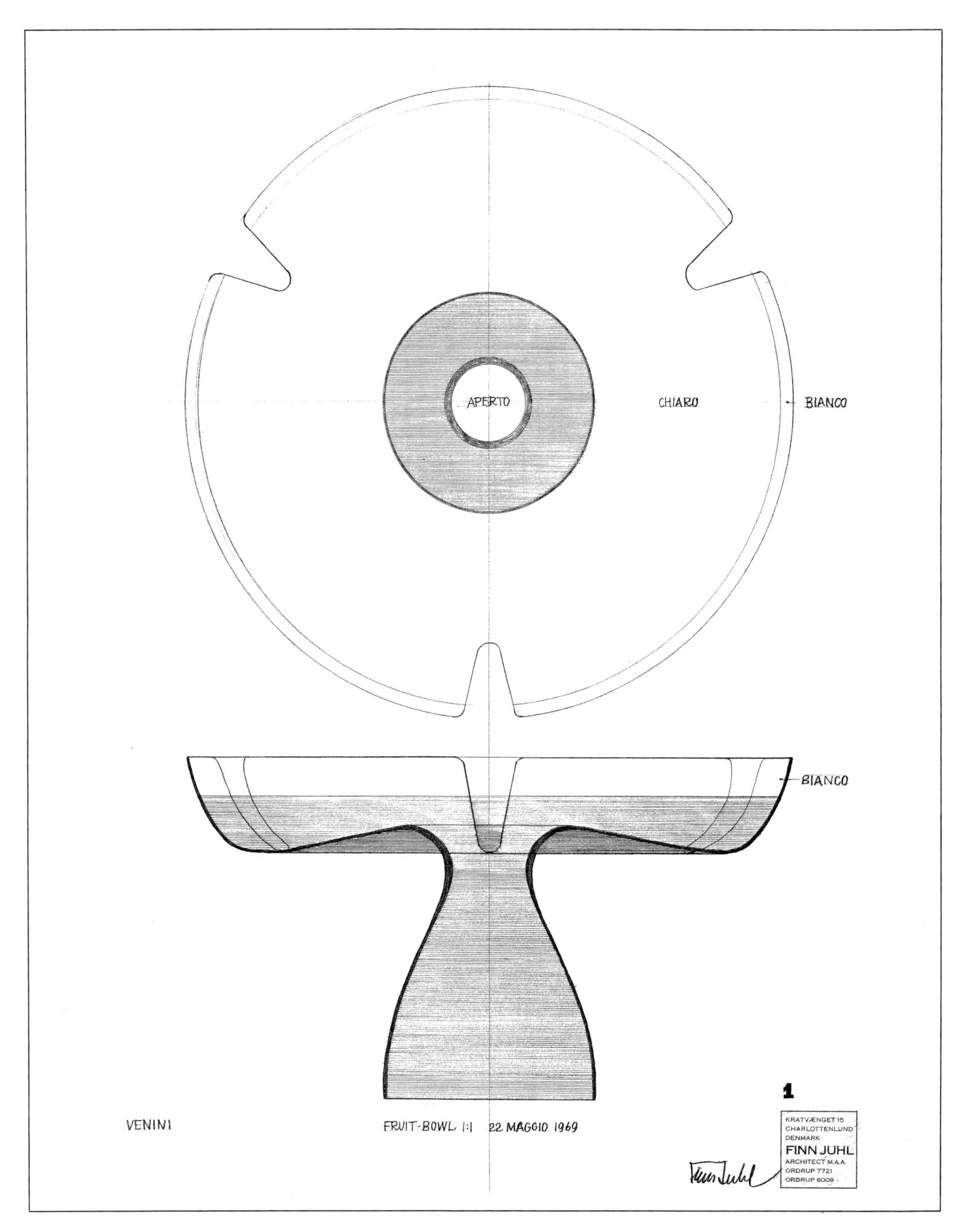

— BIANCO

VENINI   FRUIT-BOWL 1:1   22 MAGGIO 1969

1

KRATVÆNGET 15
CHARLOTTENLUND
DENMARK
FINN JUHL
ARCHITECT M.A.A.
ORDRUP 7721
ORDRUP 6009

With his unfailing eye for color, it was also natural for Finn Juhl to make designs for rugs. In 1953, he designed "Domino" rugs for Unika Væv. The rugs were made in a standard size, 70×140 cm., and could be combined to make larger carpets. He had gotten this idea from Japanese houses, where the floors are covered with tatami mats in a specific size. The rugs were backed with rubber, so that they clung to the floor and did not have to be sewn together. Their geometrical patterns could be used to create many different variations.

Later Finn Juhl made other designs for Unika Væv, but none was produced. A series of rugs – both flat-woven and long-pile – that he designed for Wittrup in Vejen was never produced, either.

What was manufactured, however, was a series of practical and lovely utilitarian objects made of wood, melamine, and metal, designed for Ørskov & Co. from 1954 to 1956. Their distinctive and timeless design would make them admirably suited to production to this very day.

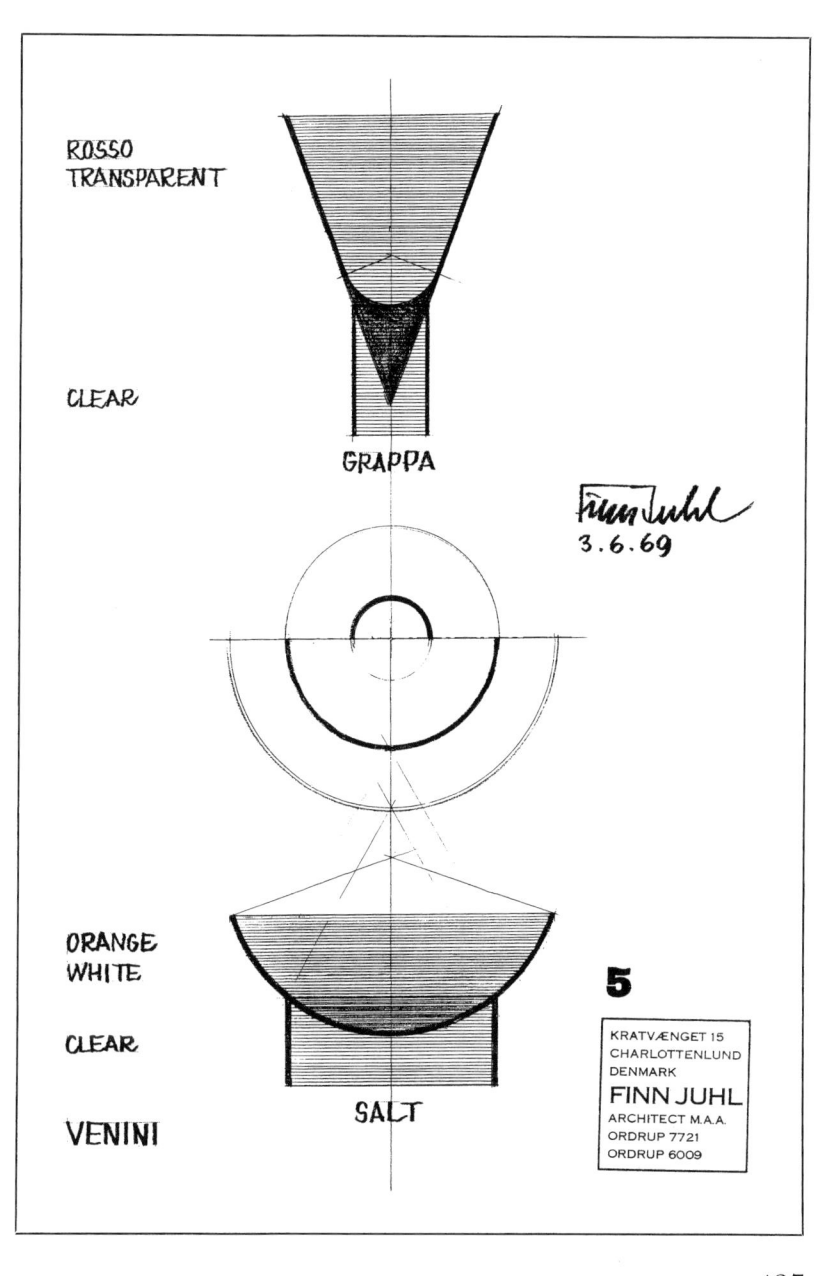

Opposite page: Design for a fruit-bowl made for Venini in 1969. Here shown on a scale of 1:2.5
This page: Design for a glass for grappa (Italian brandy) and salt cellar made for Venini in 1969. Scale, 1:2.

STRÜWING

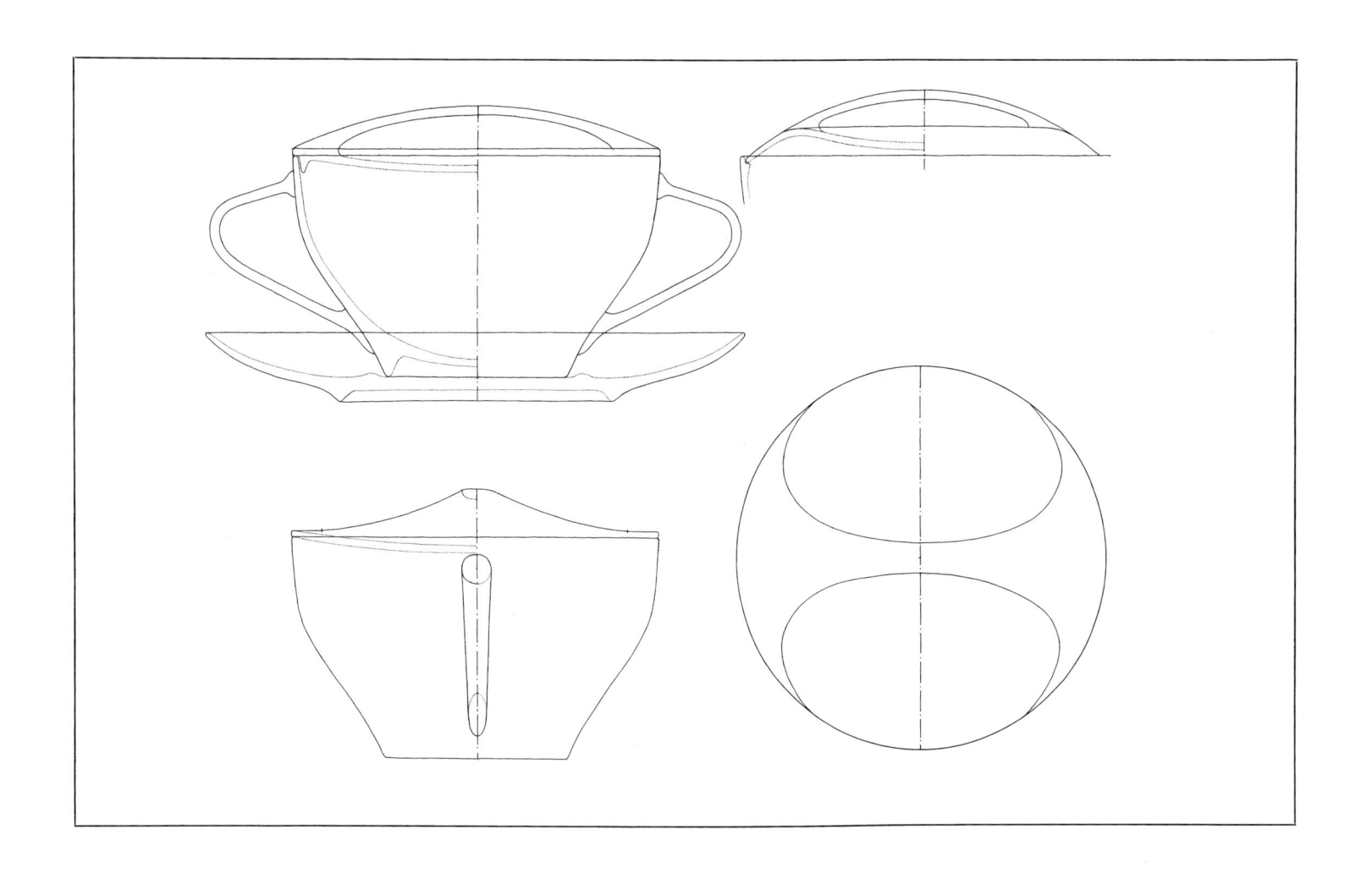

This spread: Parts of a porcelain service designed for Bing & Grøndahl in 1950–52. Scale, 1:2. Models were made of several parts of the service, but the project was abandoned nonetheless.

129

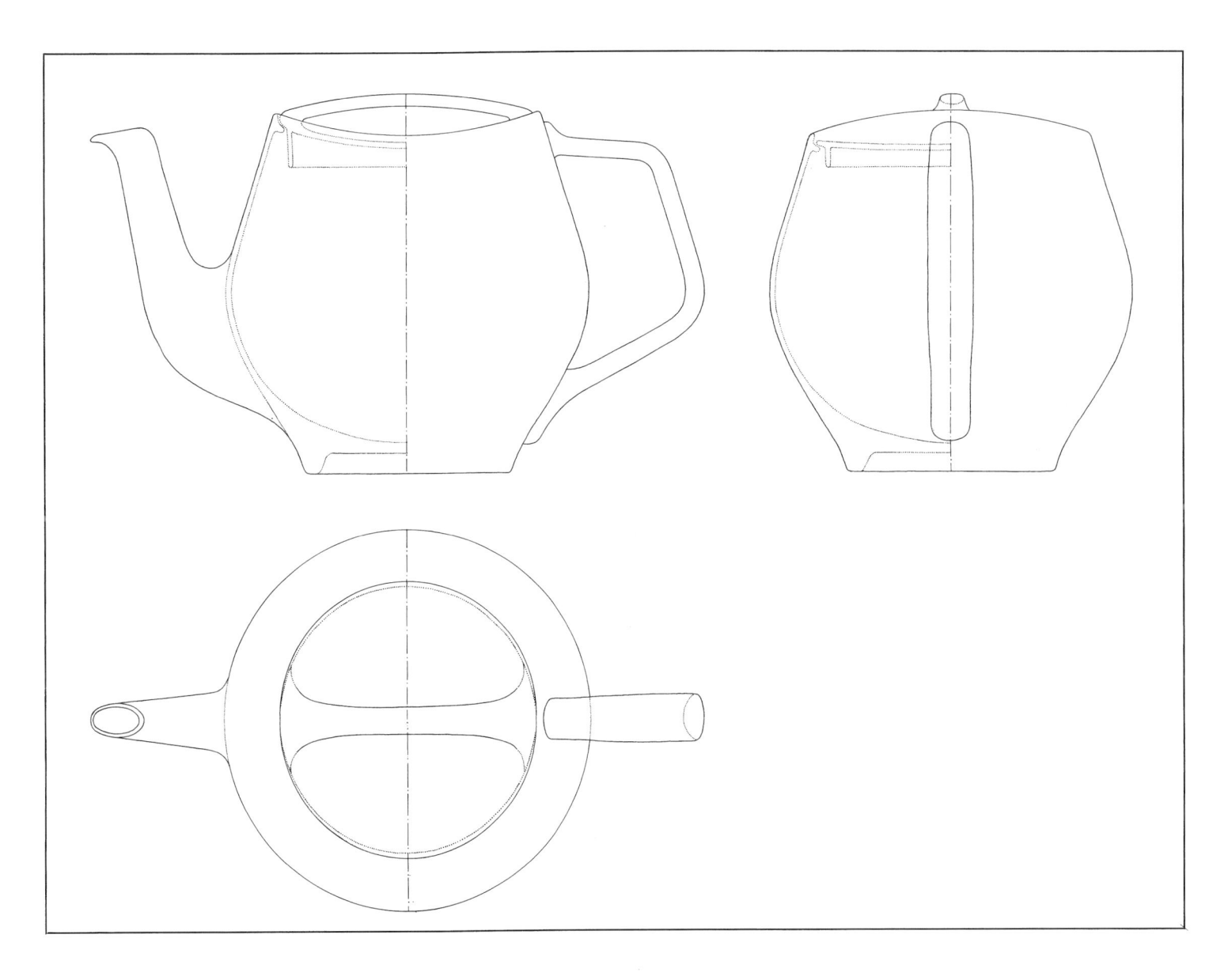

130

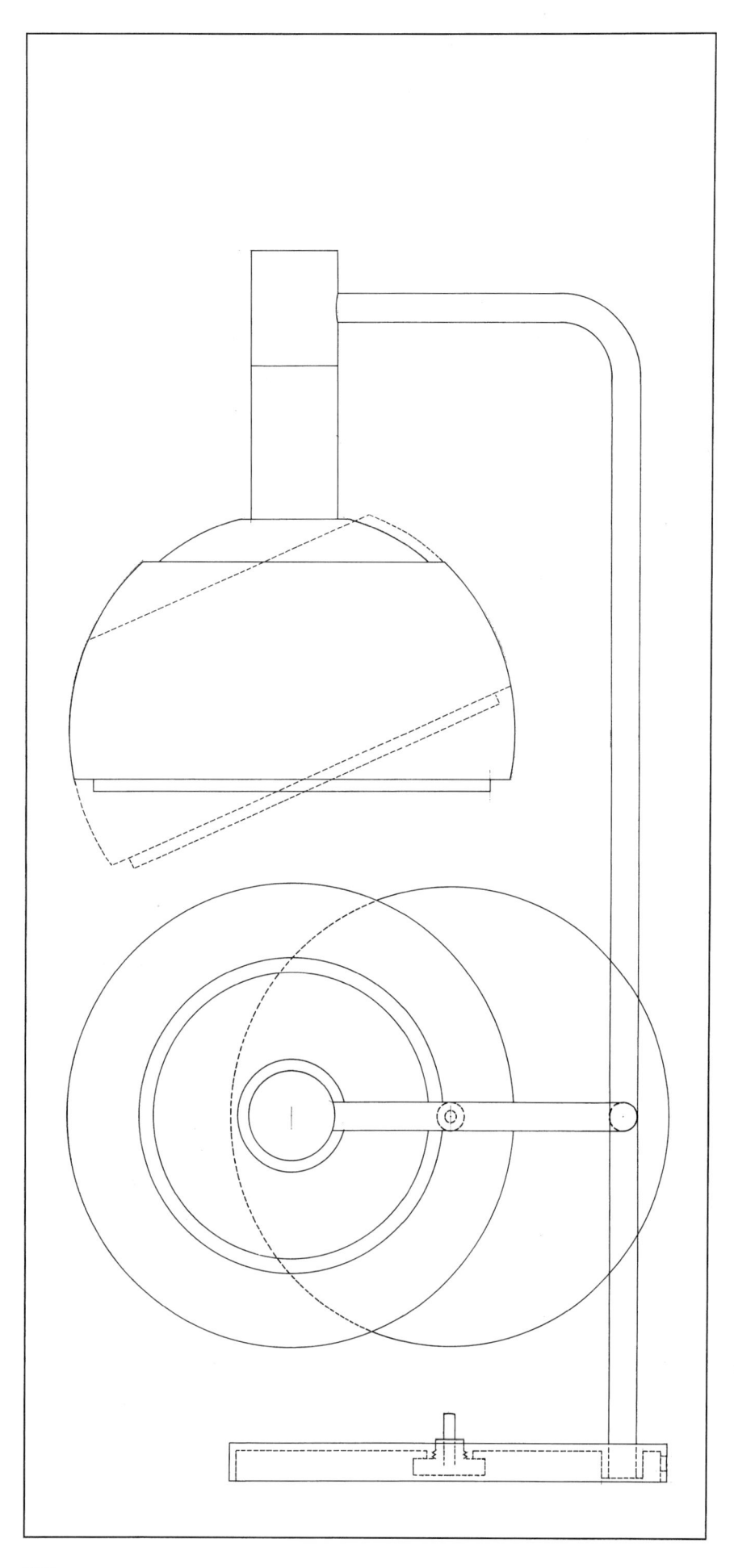

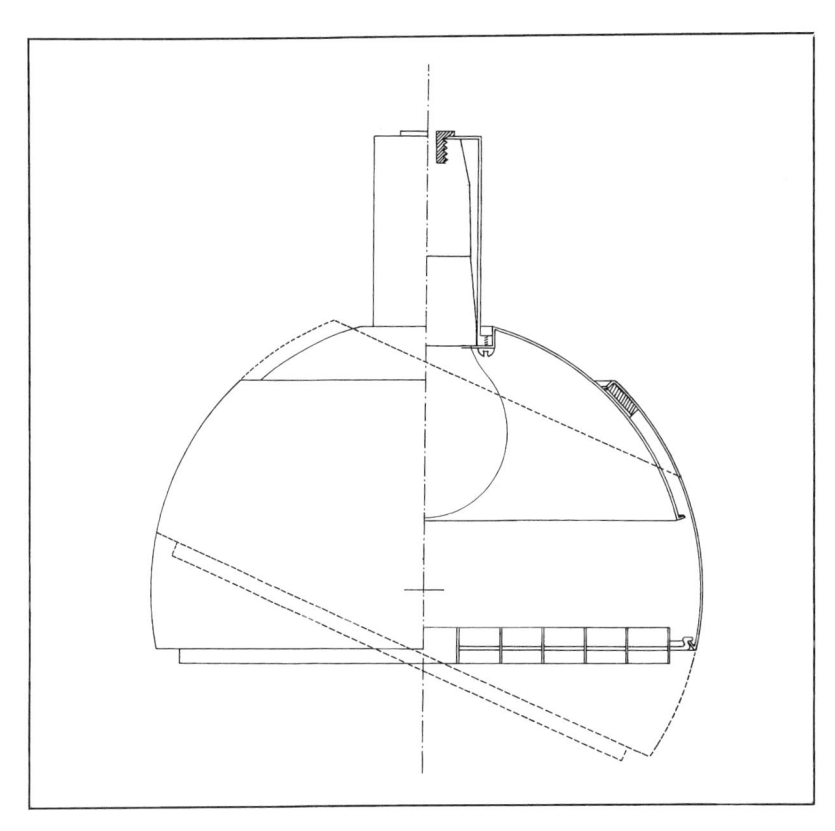

OLE WOLDBYE

This spread: Table lamp and hanging lamp designed in 1963 and manufactured by Lyfa. The lower part of the shade can be turned diagonally to change the direction of the light. The drawings are given on a scale of 1:2.

131

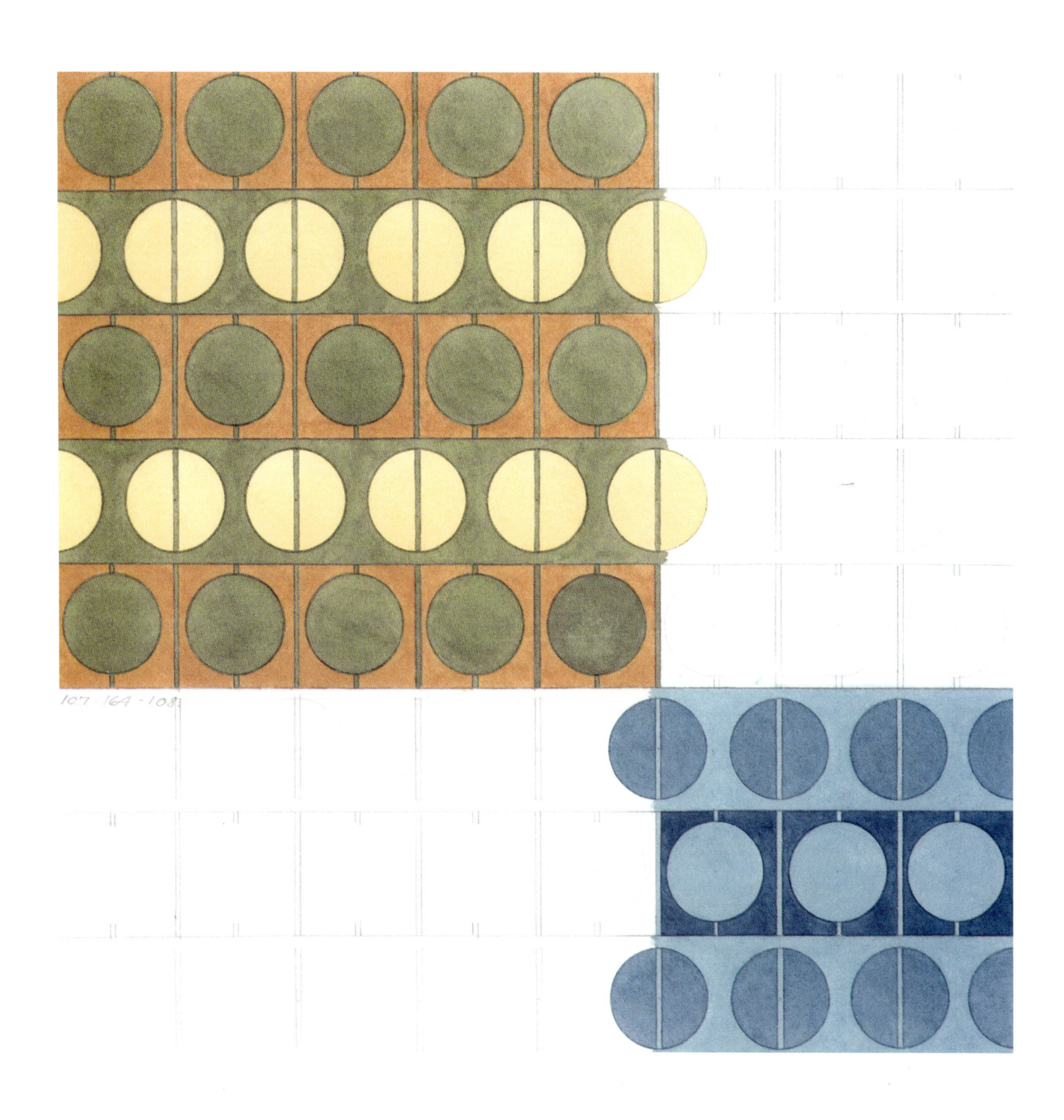

This page: Models for flat-woven rugs made for Wittrups Fabrikker in Vejen in 1963.
Opposite page: Models for long-pile rugs also made for Wittrups Fabrikker in Vejen in 1963.

133

KELD HELMER-PETERSEN

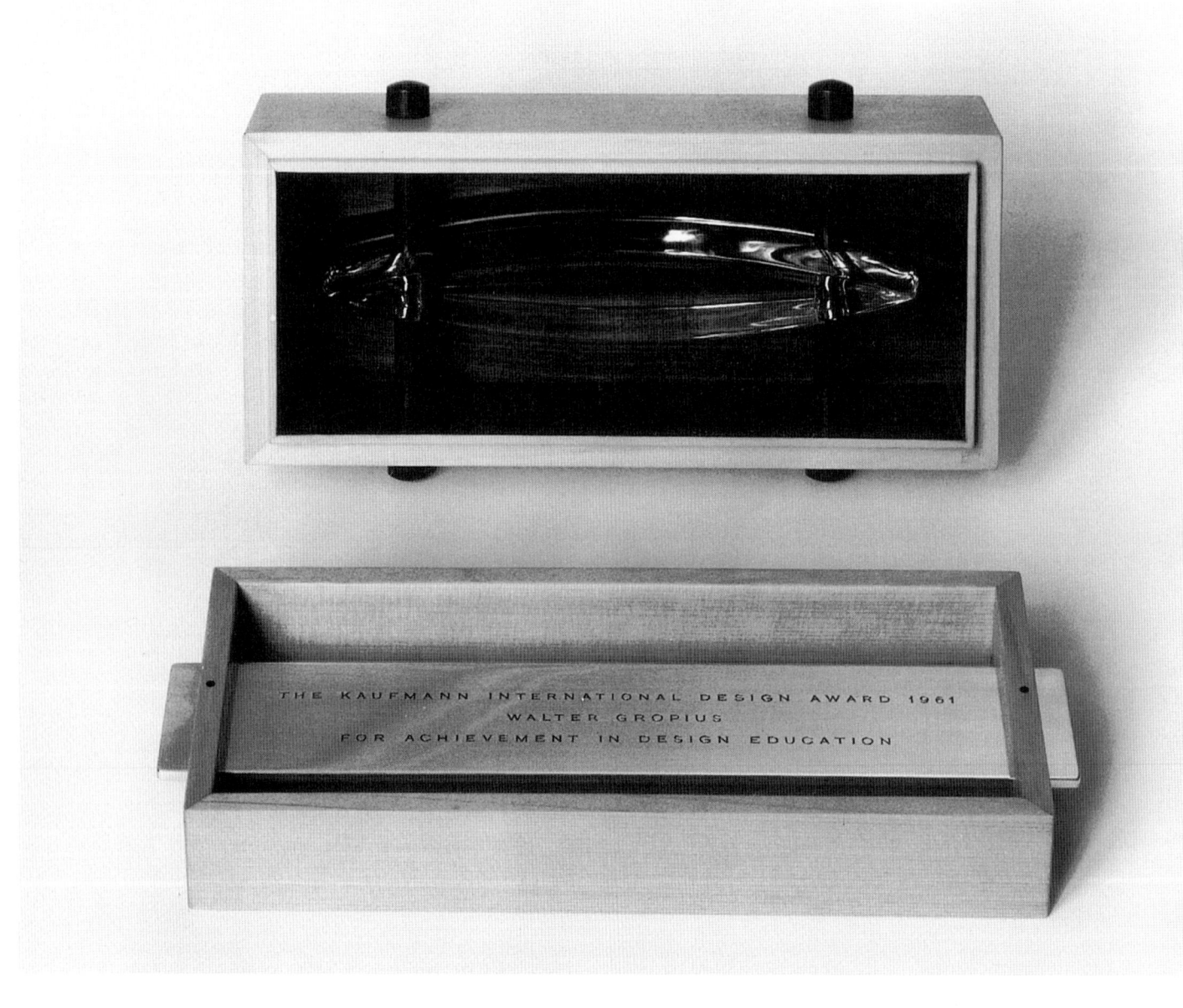

TROPHIES

The Kaufmann International Design Award

Edgar Kaufmann, Jr., founded the Kaufmann International Design Award in 1960, an honor that brought with it no less than $20,000, a considerable sum at the time. The award was to be given to persons, organizations, or groups of persons who had made an especially significant contribution within industrial design, either through their own work or through education.

The same year, Kaufmann asked Finn Juhl to design a trophy or symbol to be given to the recipient together with the award. It was a difficult task, especially since the prize and trophy would be conferred on the most renowned masters of the art of design. Finn Juhl consequently created something that both played on international *symbolism* and linked the old with the new.

He chose an object, an ancient Chinese symbol, *Yüan-Kuei*. It is a ritual hammer or axe that symbolizes the highest authority, and was conferred by the ancient Chinese emperors as a mark of favor. In China, the symbol was made of jade, but Finn Juhl chose to have it made of crystal, by Orrefors Glassworks in Sweden.

The crystal symbol was placed in a box of hinoki wood, from a tree considered holy in Japan and thus traditionally used only for palaces and temples. Its structure resembles that of Oregon pine, but it does not take on a reddish hue under the influence of light, as Oregon pine does. The lid of the box has a silver plate for engraving. The bottom part of the box, which holds the crystal symbol, is painted deep blue, and the bottom is of palisander shaped to hold the symbol in place. The symbol is spindle-shaped with rounded ends, and ebony sticks hold it in place. The box was exquisitely executed by cabinetmaker J. Pontoppidan of the rare wood, which SAS obtained in Japan and flew to Copenhagen. The silver plate and engraving were carried out by the Georg Jensen silversmithy.

Finn Juhl's goal was to create an object which was both beautiful and unique, one which possessed rich textural effects, yet still remained simple.

The award was conferred the same year on the American designers Charles and Ray Eames. After the ceremony, which Finn Juhl was unable to attend, he received the following telegram: THANK YOU DEAR FINN IT IS BEAUTIFULLY CONCEIVED AND BEAUTIFULLY EXECUTED AND WE ARE GRATEFUL FOR YOUR LOVING CARE AND SAD THAT YOU WERE NOT THERE WITH US TO SHARE THE OCCASION AND THE WARM FEELING = CHARLES AND RAY.

In 1961, the award was given to the architect *Walter Gropius*, the old Bauhaus pioneer, and in 1962 to *Olivetti* in Milan, for its excellent use of design. No more crystal symbols were awarded thereafter; the

Opposite page: The Kaufmann trophy. Above, the trophy itself, made of crystal; below, the box with the trophy placed inside and the silver plate with an inscription to Walter Gropius, who received the award in 1961.

Design for the Kaufmann trophy on a scale of 1:3.

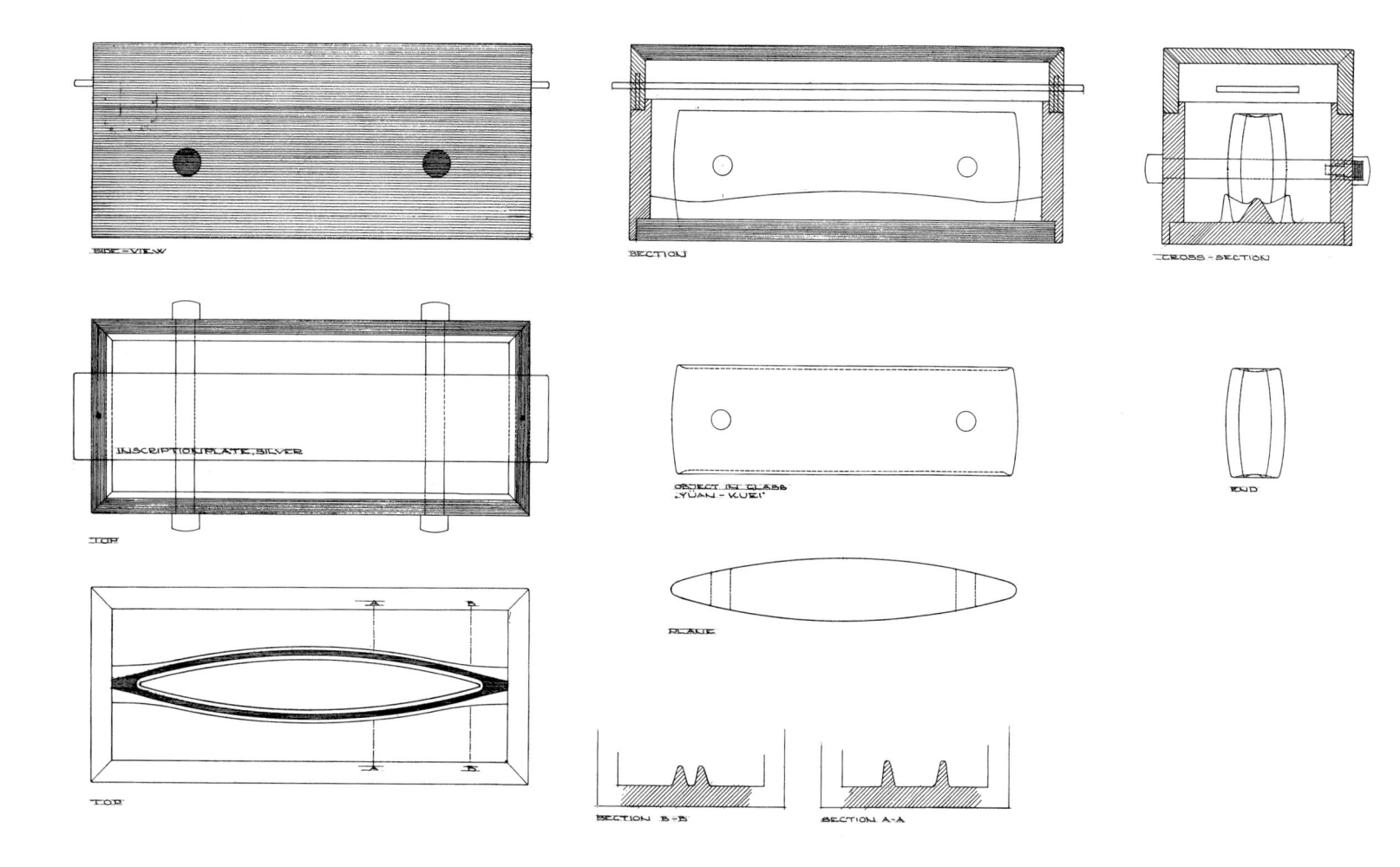

Foundation's statutes were changed so that the money was to be used for education in design. Four boxes with the symbol had been made, however. The fourth was later conferred on Germany's Wolkswagenwerk on a special occasion.

An "Export Oscar"

In addition to the trophy for the Kaufmann International Design Award, Finn Juhl designed an entry in 1966 for the National Association for Danish Enterprise's competition for a Danish "Export Oscar." It was conceived as an award to be given to companies or individuals abroad in recognition of excellent work in promoting Danish products and consequently trade between their own country and Denmark.

Finn Juhl's entry was a palisander cube base, with a circular silver inscription plate, bearing a maple bowl holding a polished steel ball. The trophy was thus made up solely of geometrical shapes: a cube, a circle, a sphere, and a semicircle, perfect basic forms combined into a harmonious entity in absolute balance. If one wanted to interpret the trophy as symbolic in any way, one could consider the ball as the earth, but Finn Juhl had wanted solely to create an object that was distinctive both visually and in its treatment of material.

The entry won second prize so only one copy of it was made, the one Finn Juhl sent in to the competition. The first prize was awarded

136

Entry for the National Association for Danish Enterprise competition for an "Export Oscar" in 1966. The circular silver plate was intended for an inscription.

to a ceramic sculpture in the form of a sprouting seed. In contrast to Finn Juhl's entry, it was unable to bear an inscription (something specified in the competition rules), and thus had to be accompanied by a diploma.

CONCLUSION

It has often been written that Finn Juhl won international acclaim before he was recognized in his own country. And it is a good story: he first went through such awful tribulations – and then he became famous! But as we now know, the story is not true. Like everything new, his first furniture was indeed met with scepticism, but criticism was often well founded. From the middle of the 1940s, criticism was already overwhelmingly positive, in fact appreciative. It was obvious that he, Wegner, and a few others had brought about necessary regeneration. The attack from Karlsen and Mogensen did not come until 1962, so he was able to take it in his stride – something he in fact did. At this point, his importance had been recognized from almost all quarters.

In other fields, too, he was successful from the time he had established himself as an independent architect. He was awarded the C.F. Hansen prize for young architects for his own house in 1943, and as early as 1947, received the Eckersberg Medal for his first major interior commission, Bing & Grøndahl. The Trusteeship Council Chamber in New York was a distinguished official commission, one which he received without ever having carried out any official project in Denmark. And the industrial manufacture of his furniture was started at around the same time both in the United States and in Denmark. So it is not correct that his furniture first had to catch on in the United States before the Danish furniture industry dared tackle it.

It is naturally true that in his early years Finn Juhl was not on good terms with the established Danish furniture tradition, whose strong man was Kaare Klint, and that the Museum of Decorative Art, where Klint was highly influential, was late to include his furniture in its collections, something that did not happen until 1952. But there was no personal animosity between Finn Juhl and Kaare Klint. They did not even know one another personally, though Finn Juhl mentioned at one point that they had met on a social occasion, at a gathering after the opening of an exhibition of work by Aino and Alvar Aalto at the Museum of Decorative Art in 1948. The author, who designed this exhibition, was present and witnessed the discussion. He remembers that Klint actually showed no little sympathy for Finn Juhl's favorite idea: the link between the fine art of the day and furniture design. Bent Salicath wrote about this in 1972. "In Kaare Klint's latest years, he had a clearer understanding of Finn Juhl's completely different world of form. Kaare Klint was also musical and was frequently present at the chamber music society's intimate concerts. Finn Juhl, in turn, also understood more of the sturdy Bachian tones in Kaare Klint's logically-built rhythms in furniture. Two musical furniture designers with many conflicting views met at last with some understanding of one another's different qualities where they were expressed so sonorously in creating art through furniture and in rooms with highly diverse compositions."[17]

But Finn Juhl was in principal an opponent of "schools" because in his view they adopt a certain idiom and limit creativity. Though he himself was a senior teacher at a school of interior design, he earnestly tried to avoid producing little "Finn Juhls." He let his students work freely with their projects, and he exerted his influence as a teacher by critically reviewing them. One of his students wrote that he was hardly a good teacher in the present sense of the word. "If I must use a modern word for Finn Juhl's relation to us students, the word 'guru' would probably come closest. He was world famous, had a fancy American car, was well dressed, knew how to formulate himself, and was able to get what he wanted – all things that actually would be perfectly immaterial if he had not in addition been able to give us something that is difficult to define but which resulted in us having a sense of how to make everyday life more beautiful, while knowing that this esthetic should be based on the functional aspect – the bearing and borne – for which his furniture has been an expression through the years."[18]

Finn Juhl was born on the sunny side of life, and the sun shone on him almost throughout his days. His extensive work in the United States and later in Europe and Asia for SAS made him into a cosmopolitan. He was gifted in languages, knowledgeable, especially about architecture and art, elegant in appearance (not without a touch of arrogance); he made acquaintances easily, something which often led to life-long friendships. He was famous, and he would also have been a wretch if he had not enjoyed it – but he did!

Everywhere he went on his many travels, he expanded his knowledge of art in all its forms, both the art of today and that of yesterday. As a connoisseur, he was perhaps more selective than actually fastidious. The former director of the Museum of Decorative Art, Erik Lassen, tells of a characteristic feature in this respect: "Many years ago, I had the experience of being Finn Juhl's cicerone at the Louvre. He fell in love with an early Greek statue and did not want to see anything else."[19]

His house on Kratvænget bordered on Ordrupgaard Museum's park, and in his later years, over the hedge, he met the museum's director, the art historian Haavard Rostrup, and his wife Vibeke. The result was one of the fruitful friendships that was characteristic of Finn Juhl. Rostrup was also a discerning gentleman when it came to art, and together they often went on little excursions to museums and exhibitions, followed by lively discussions.

After a divorce from his first wife, Finn Juhl started life together with the music publisher Hanne Wilhelm Hansen in 1961. And this is how a new dimension in his life opened up in earnest: music. Since 1959, she had been a partner in the old respected music publishing house, Wilhelm Hansen, which in addition to publishing, was also actively engaged in arranging concerts. Through Hanne Wilhelm Hansen's work, Finn Juhl made close contacts with the international music world. He often accompanied her on trips abroad and was naturally an excellent host at her side when famous artists came on concert tours to Denmark. This suited him very well during the many years after he had completely relinquished his work as an architect, especially since he had always had a weakness for celebrities.

It is strange that almost all of Finn Juhl's work within architecture and interior design is gone. The large exhibitions have vanished as a matter of course. The Bing & Grøndahl store as he remodeled it no longer exists, either. The Trusteeship Council Chamber in New York has been changed beyond recognition. Villabyernes Bio was torn down. SAS's foreign ticket offices have all been redone. The fine DC-8s have long since been replaced. The Hotel Richmond restaurant has been remodeled. Only his own house and a few others that he built remain, and probably only his own home remains completely unchanged.

But his furniture has not disappeared. It stands in museums the world over and in innumerable homes. Some of his best models from the days of the Cabinetmakers' Guild are being produced once again – more than forty years after they were designed. When he presented them for the first time at the Cabinetmakers' Guild exhibitions they were controversial: today they are modern classics.

FOOTNOTES
1. Interview in Politiken, November 9, 1982. - 2. Arkitektens Ugehefte, 1939, p. 190. - 3. Politiken, November 5, 1982. - 4. Arkitektens Ugehefte, 1946, p. 113. - 5. Probably written in 1955. It was not possible to find where the article, which was found in transcript in Finn Juhl's archives, was published. It is not mentioned in Edgar Kaufmann's bibliography in *9 Commentaries on Frank Lloyd Wright*, New York, 1989. - 6. Letter dated October 22, 1969, in Finn Juhl's archives. - 7. Nyt Tidskrift for Kunstindustri, 1947, pp. 109-121. - 8. Arkitektens Ugehefte, 1945, pp. 173-175. - 9. Nyt Tidskrift for Kunstindustri, 1948, pp. 172-176. - 10. Dansk Kunsthaandværk, 1959, pp. 162-177. - 11. Arkitektens Ugehefte, 1962, pp. 1-11. - 12. Dansk Kunsthaandværk, 1962, pp. 181-189. - 13. Yearbook of the Nordenfjeldske Museum of Applied Art, 1950, p. 20. - 14. Dansk Kunsthaandværk, 1949, pp. 56-60. - 15. Dansk Brugskunst, 1972, pp. 53-55. - 16. Yearbook of the Nordenfjeldske Museum of Applied Art, 1950, p. 17. - 17. Dansk Brugskunst, 1972, pp. 53-55. - 18. Rum og Form, 1981, p. 22. - 19. Catalogue of the Finn Juhl exhibition at the Museum of Decorative Art, 1982.

Finn Juhl – Curriculum vitæ

Born on January 30, 1912, in Copenhagen, Denmark.
Graduated from Sct. Jørgens Gymnasium, 1930.
Studied at the Royal Danish Academy of Fine Arts, School of Architecture, 1930–34.
Employed by the architect Vilhelm Lauritzen, 1934–45.
Debut with furniture at the Cabinetmakers' Guild exhibitions, 1937.
Furniture models for cabinetmaker Niels Vodder, 1937–59.
Married Inge-Marie Skaarups on July 15, 1937 (later divorced).
Membership in the Academic Architects Association (now the Federation of Danish Architects).
Built his house on Kratvænget, 1942.
C.F. Hansen prize for young architects, 1943.
Independent design office in Nyhavn opened, 1945.
Senior teacher at the School of Interior Design, 1945–55.
Designed Bing & Grøndahl store on Amagertorv Square, 1946.
Eckersberg Medal, 1947.
Svend Schaumann's florist's shop, Kongens Nytorv, 1948.
"Contemporary Danish Architecture" exhibition, London, 1950.
Danish Handcraft Guild exhibition, London, 1950.
Mrs. Anthon Petersen's summer house in Asserbo, 1950.
"Good Design" exhibition, Chicago, 1951.
Designed the Trusteeship Council Chamber, U.N. Headquarters, New York, 1951–52.
Furniture ranges for Baker Furniture, Inc., Grand Rapids, Michigan, 1951–55.
Furniture ranges for Bovirke, Copenhagen, 1952–64.
Furniture ranges for France & Daverkosen, Ørholm, and France & Søn, Hillerød, 1953–69.
"Angewandte Kunst aus Dänemark" exhibition, Zurich, 1952.
Remodeled the Georg Jensen store on Fifth Avenue, New York, 1952.
Single-family house for M. Aubertin, Nakskov, 1952.
Designed a room with his own furniture, etc. at the Nordenfjeldske Museum of Applied Art, Trondheim, Norway, 1952.
"Home of the Future" exhibition at the Cabinetmakers' Guild 400th anniversary exhibition at Forum, 1954.
Georg Jensen silversmithy, 50th anniversary exhibition, Museum of Decorative Art, Copenhagen, 1954.
"50 Years of Danish Silver" exhibition, London, 1954; Washington, D.C., Louisville, and Dallas, 1955; and St. Louis, 1957.
Designed Denmark's stand at the Xth Triennial in Milan, 1954. Honorary diploma.
Villabyernes Bio movie theater, Vangede, 1955. Awarded a diploma by Gentofte Municipality.
Director's office for France & Daverkosen, Ørholm, 1955.
Model apartment at the H55 exhibition in Helsingborg, Sweden, 1955.
Designed SAS's ticket offices in Europe and Asia, 1956–61.
"Neue Form aus Dänemark" traveling exhibition in 8 German cities and Vienna, 1956–57.

Designed a store in Toronto for Georg Jensen, Inc., 1956.
Designed interior of DC-8 planes for SAS.
Design office moved to 38 Sølvgade, 1957.
Remodeled the Georg Jensen store on New Bond Street, London, 1957 (together with Trevor Danatt).
Denmark's stand at the XIth Triennial in Milan, 1957. Awarded a gold medal.
Furnished the ambassador's residence at the Royal Danish Embassy, Washington, D.C., 1960.
of Art, New York, 1960.
"The Arts of Denmark" exhibition moved to museums in Washington, D.C., Chicago, and Los Angeles, 1960-61.
Trophy for the Kaufmann International Design Award, 1960.
Began a common-law marriage with Hanne Wilhelm Hansen, 1961.
Summer house for Anders Hostrup-Pedersen, Raageleje, 1962.
Expansion of Bing & Grøndahl store, 1963.
A.I.D. prize for design, Chicago, 1964.
Visiting professor, Institute of Design, Chicago, 1965.
Designed the Hotel Richmond restaurant, 1965.
Remodeled the Wilhelm Hansen Musikforlag store on Gothersgade, 1966.
"Two Centuries of Danish Design" exhibition, Victoria & Albert Museum, London, 1968.
"A Century of Danish Design" exhibition, Kelvingrove Museum, Glasgow, and Whitworth Art Gallery, Manchester, 1968.
Exhibition of arts and crafts, Brussels, 1969.
Retrospective exhibition of his own work, Charlottenborg Autumn Exhibition, 1970.
Received a life-long pension from the State Budget, 1971.
Exhibition of his own work, Cantu, Italy, 1973.
Made an Honorary Royal Designer for Industry, London, 1978.
Retrospective exhibition of furniture and other work, Museum of Decorative Art, Copenhagen, 1982.
Knight of the Order of the Dannebrog, 1984.
Died, May 17, 1989.

Finn Juhl's literary work

BOOK:

Hjemmets indretning. Undated (1954).

ARTICLES:

Eget hus i Ordrup Krat, in Arkitektens Månedshefte, no. 8, 1944, pp. 121-127.

Løses lejlighedens problemer i massebyggeriet?, in Arkitektens Ugehefte, no. 45, 1946, pp. 233 and 246-247.

Møbelbogen (review), in Arkitektens Ugehefte, no. 4, 1947, p. 13.

A/S Bing & Grøndahl – butiksinventar, in Arkitektens Månedshefte, no. 8, 1947, pp. 79-84.

Bo rigtigt (review), in Arkitektens Ugehefte, no. 35, 1948, p. 147.

Fortid, nutid, fremtid, in Dansk Kunsthaandværk, no. 4, 1949, pp. 56-60.

Vilhelm Lundstrøm in memoriam, in Arkitektens Ugehefte, no. 22, 1950, pp. 103-104.

Den skabende proces, in the catalogue for the spring exhibition of the Danish Society of Arts and Crafts, 1950.

Tre danske brugskunstnere om sitt fag, in the yearbook of the Nordenfjeldske Museum of Applied Art, 1950, pp. 17-26.

Sølv (review of the spring exhibition of the Danish Society of Arts and Crafts), in Dansk Kunsthaandværk, no. 6, 1951, pp. 99-102.

Good design '51 as seen by its director and by its designer, in Interiors (U.S.A.), no. 110, 1951, pp. 100-103.

Interiør – 52, in the yearbook of the Nordenfjeldske Museum of Applied Art, 1952, pp. 93-110.

Enfamiliehus ved Nakskov fjord, in Arkitektens Månedhefte, no. 1, 1953, pp. 13-16.

Interiør – 52, in Dansk Kunsthaandværk, nol. 5, 1953, pp. 76-78.

Kunsthåndværkeren Kay Bojesen, in Dansk Kunsthaandværk, 1959, no. 3, pp. 62-65.

Om Kaufmann-prisens symbol, in Dansk Kunsthaandværk, no. 7-8, 1961, p. 159.

En egyptisk familie, feature article in Politiken, October 9, 1976.

Writings about Finn Juhl

Only books and articles with extensive treatment of Finn Juhl are included.

BOOKS:

Esbjørn Hiort: *Modern Danish Furniture* (text in Danish, English, German, French), 1956.

Henrik Sten Møller: *Dansk Design* (text in Danish and English), 1975.

Grete Jalk: *Dansk Møbelkunst gennem 40 år*, I-IV, 1987.

Henrik Sten Møller: *Fra vor egen tid – 100 års boligidealer*, 1990.

Frederik Sieck: *Contemporary Danish Furniture Design*, 1990 (English and Danish editions).

Weilbachs Kunstnerleksikon, 1949.

Dansk Kunsthåndværker Leksikon, 1979.

Dansk Biografisk, Leksikon, 1981.

ARTICLES:

Edgar Kaufmann, Jr,: *Finn Juhl of Copenhagen*, in Interiors (U.S.A.), No. 108, 1948, pp. 96-99.

Edgar Kaufmann, Jr,: *Good design '51 as seen by its director and by its designer,* in Interiors (U.S.A.), no. 110, 1951, pp. 100-103.

The three council chambers of the United Nations, in Interiors (U.S.A.), no. 12, 1952, pp. 45-67.

Bent Salicath: *Finn Juhl and Danish Furniture*, in Architects' Yearbook, no. 6, 1955, pp. 37-57.

Martin Hartung: *Finn Juhl i Mobilia Club*, in Mobilia, no. 117, 1965, pp. 9-34.

Bent Salicath: *Finn Juhl – manden med de følsomme fingre*, in Dansk Brugskunst, no. 2, 1972, pp. 53-55.

Frederik Sieck: *Finn Juhl*, in Mobilia, no. 251/252, 1976, pp. 47-56.

Mike Rømer (ed.): *Rundt om Finn Juhl*, in Rum og Form, no. 4, 1981, pp. 6-27.

Esbjørn Hiort: *Finn Juhl 1912-1989* (obituary), in Arkitekten, no. 14, 1989, pp. 356-357.

Kirsten Dovey: *Formens elegantier,* feature article in Politiken, February 16, 1990.

Mike Rømer: *Finn Juhl hædres med udstillinger og bøger*, in Arkitekten, no. 5, 1990, p. 176.

CATALOGUES:

Finn Juhl – møbler og andre arbejder, Museum of Decorative Art, Copenhagen, 1982.

Finn Juhl Memorial Exhibition, Osaka, Japan, 1990.

INDEX TO RECORDS:

Esbjørn Hiort: *Registrant over arkitekt Finn Juhls tegninger,* 1990 (copies at the Museum of Decorative Art, Copenhagen).